D0431778

Jan 18

THE
CANADALAND
GUIDE TO CANADA

(PUBLISHED IN AMERICA)

JESSE BROWN

WITH VICKY MOCHAMA AND NICK ZARZYCKI

TOUCHSTONE

New York   London   Toronto   Sydney   New Delhi

Touchstone
An Imprint of Simon & Schuster, Inc.
1230 Avenue of the Americas
New York, NY 10020

First Touchstone edition May 2017

TOUCHSTONE and colophon are registered trademarks of Simon & Schuster, Inc.

For information about special discounts for bulk purchases, please contact Simon & Schuster Special Sales at 1-866-506-1949 or business@simonandschuster.com.

The Simon & Schuster Speakers Bureau can bring authors to your live event. For more information or to book an event, contact the Simon & Schuster Speakers Bureau at 1-866-248-3049 or visit our website at www.simonspeakers.com.

Manufactured in the United States of America

1 3 5 7 9 10 8 6 4 2

ISBN 978-1-5011-5063-0
ISBN 978-1-5011-5065-4 (ebook)

For Jesse Brown

THE
CANADALAND
GUIDE TO CANADA

(PUBLISHED IN AMERICA)

by Jesse Brown

with Vicky Mochama and Nick Zarzycki

Editors: Nita Pronovost and Brendan May

Designer: Paul Bucci

Cover Painting: Dan Buller

Cover Design: Paul Barker

Illustrators: Andrew Barr, Deshi Deng

Contributors: Kathryn Borel, Rachel Bulatovich, Winnie Code, Melissa Deleary, Jacob Duarte Spiel, Aaron Hagey-MacKay, Jill Krajewski, Dave McGimpsey, Alex Nursall, Emma Overton, Simren Sandhu, Alexander Saxton, John Semley, Samuel Smith, Jimmy Thomson, Jamie Whitecrow, Bryce Warnes

CONTENTS

HOW TO BEHAVE

HOW WE THINK

HOW WE MAKE A LIVING

HOW TO READ THIS BOOK

The blue stuff over here in italics is silly nonsense.

What you're reading right now is the main body text of *The Canadaland Guide to Canada*. Despite the swears and made-up words like "bonerish," the stuff over here is real, so far as we can tell. We looked it up. I mean, we didn't call up the people involved or dig up old diaries from tombs or anything. But we didn't just copy and paste it from Wikipedia, either. We got it mostly from books and old newspaper articles. Look, maybe there's a mistake in here, who knows? But the idea is that this stuff is real.

QUOTE**SQUARE**

"Yes, the person quoted in these boxes actually said or wrote this stuff. In this case, it was me, Nick." —Nick Zarzycki

IS THIS SHIT REAL?

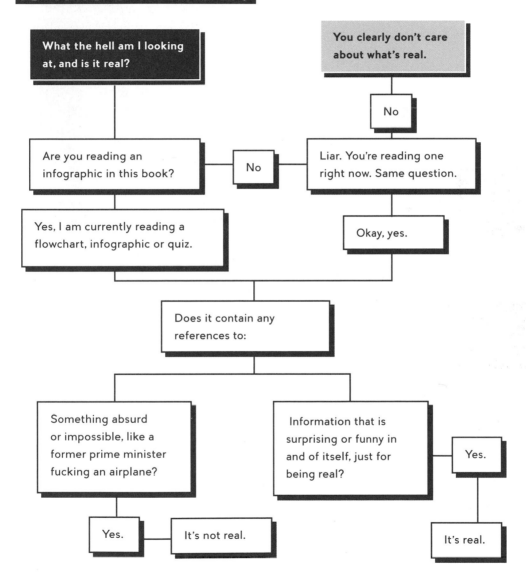

What the hell am I looking at, and is it real?

You clearly don't care about what's real.

No

Are you reading an infographic in this book?

No

Liar. You're reading one right now. Same question.

Yes, I am currently reading a flowchart, infographic or quiz.

Okay, yes.

Does it contain any references to:

Something absurd or impossible, like a former prime minister fucking an airplane?

Information that is surprising or funny in and of itself, just for being real?

Yes.

Yes.

It's not real.

It's real.

INTRODUCTION

CANADA: A BEIGE NATION

Quick—picture Canada.

Not the forest. The tiny strip along the bottom where people live. The cities. Think about what they look like.

Now, consider Canadians. Think about their clothes. Try to remember what their accents sound like.

Coming up empty? Is everything "Canada" blurring together into a shapeless, beige haze?

That's exactly what we're going for. Normalcy is the gold standard in Canada. Our aspirations are generic. We aim to pass. If you can't distinguish Vancouver from Seattle or Toronto from Frankfurt, we're thrilled.

The only thing that would give us more pleasure would be if you considered us to be just like you, but a little better.

Not in a flashy way. We're not talking about better looking, or smarter, or richer, or more skilled. Just . . . a little cleaner. A little nicer. Feel free to cite us as an example of how your progressive politics aren't so crazy after all. Diversity! Gun control! Free health care! Abortions! No big deal up in Canada, right?

We share a border with America. When your next-door neighbor is a billionaire crackhead porn star with a machine gun, you can get away with all kinds of shit and nobody will ever notice.

You can dig up the world's dirtiest oil and be known as environmentalists! You can sell billions of dollars of weapons to murderous tyrants and be known as peacekeepers! You can deprive Indigenous people of clean drinking water and be known as multiculturalists!

In reality, Canadians don't say "eh" or call each other "hoser" or eat more donuts than Americans (we do eat a shit-ton of donuts, though). We are more polite, but we are far less kind. We'll choose peace and order over freedom any day of the week.

We enjoy our benign stereotype as much as anyone. Probably more so, since we're the ones who created it. But it's time we grew up and told the truth.

Sorry!

THE BASICS

Macdonald was still 30 percent less drunk and racist than everyone else in the country at the time.

OUR DRUNK, RACIST DAD

Macdonald loved Canada, but like most people, he loved alcohol more.

No man is more credited with the birth of our nation than our first prime minister, Sir John A. Macdonald. He united four British colonies into a single dominion and built an epic railway to connect them. He did all this while drunkenly extolling the virtues of the Aryan race, binge drinking his way through federal elections, puking during speeches, intentionally starving "Indians," and setting himself on fire.

TIMELINE OF DRUNKENNESS

1822

A psychotic babysitter forces seven-year-old Macdonald and his five-year-old brother to guzzle gin, then kills his brother with a cane.

1866

Macdonald travels to London to lobby Queen Victoria for Canadian sovereignty. He nearly burns himself to death in his hotel room when he passes out near a lit candle, probably while hammered.

1866

Canada is invaded by veterans of the American Civil War. Macdonald, leader of the colony's militia, spends the entire attack fabulously drunk in his office.

ACHIEVEMENTS

FEMINIST

Macdonald introduced a progressive bill to extend voting rights to unmarried, propertied women—the best kind of women. When members of the House protested, he quickly edited the bill to remove the votes-for-women bit.

Macdonald likely introduced the bill on a dare.

MODEL RAILWAY HOBBYIST

Macdonald worked tirelessly to build a full-scale model of the Canadian Pacific Railway connecting Vancouver to Montréal.

INDIAN AFFAIRS MINISTER

Macdonald passed the Indian Act, set up the residential schools system and bragged about keeping tribes "on the verge of actual starvation" by killing their buffalo, so that he could hustle them away from his railway ("verge" shmerge, many were in fact starved to death). Also, he had Métis hero Louis Riel hanged.

INFOBOX

Sir John A. Macdonald's name is included, for unclear reasons, in a historical database of British slave owners.

1872

Macdonald spends the entire federal election "more or less under the influence of wine." Wins a majority government.

1872

In a drunken stupor, Macdonald writes a desperate plea for bribe money to railway contractors. "I must have another ten thousand," he begs. "Do not fail me; answer today."

1883

Macdonald secures the "Intoxicating Liquors Bill," giving the government Al Capone-level control of liquor distribution in Canada, which it holds to this day.

The Queen refers to all her Canadian subjects as "sweetie."

Dogs and horses report that the feeling is mutual.

OUR ESTRANGED, INFIRM BRITISH MOTHER

Canada's head of state is an old British lady named Elizabeth who has never lived in Canada, enjoys the company of dogs and horses, and derives all her power directly from the will of God. She lives in a palace in London, is commander-in-chief of Australia's military, and runs the Church of England. Canadians who care about the monarchy simply relish the thought of submitting themselves to a powerful British mother figure. She exists mainly to comfort Canadians who miss colonialism.

INFO**BOX**

Canada is the only European monarchy visible from the moon.

A GUIDE TO INTERACTING WITH CANADA'S HEAD OF STATE

NO TOUCHING

When Elizabeth first visited Canada in 1951, members of the press were forbidden to approach "within a distance of fifteen feet" and from speaking to her unless first addressed by her. Royal protocol strongly discourages any touching. When Canadian cyclist Louis Garneau put his hand around the Queen's shoulder for a photograph in 2002, it made national headlines in the UK.

To be fair, no Canadian has ever been interested in touching the Queen either.

IF YOU STARTLE HER, YOU'LL GO TO JAIL

The Canadian Criminal Code explicitly forbids committing an act with an intent to "alarm Her Majesty." The offense is punishable by a prison term of up to two years.

Things that alarm the Queen: the lower orders, Prince Charles.

KILL ANYONE ELSE, JUST NOT HER MAJESTY

Conspiring to kill the Canadian prime minister is not considered treason according to the Criminal Code of Canada. It is treason only if you conspire against the Queen.

THE QUEEN'S VARIOUS ROLES

MASCOT/GOOD LUCK CHARM

The Canadian government gets very defensive when describing the Queen. "We do not swear allegiance to a piece of cloth (office), a document (a constitution) or a political entity. Rather we swear allegiance to a person who embodies . . . our collective values as a people."

WARRIOR FOR JESUS

The Queen is an extremely vocal Christian. In 2000, she said that "the teachings of Christ and my own personal accountability before God provide a framework in which I try to lead my life." She is Supreme Governor of the Church of England and her official title in Canada is "Defender of the Faith." No one has been able to explain how this is compatible with Canada's system of secular democracy (probably because it isn't).

CABBAGE

Other likely favorite games include: Need for Speed VII: Equestrian; Call of Duty: Boer War; Wii Normal Person Chore Simulator.

People close to Elizabeth reportedly call her "cabbage." She is also apparently "addicted" to Nintendo Wii, and was sent a custom gold-plated console by Nintendo. Favorite game: Wii Bowling.

MONARCHISTS

A small minority of Canadians want Canada to have the monarchy forever. Monarchists dearly miss the good old days of colonialism, stage protests whenever someone wants to remove the Queen's face from a stamp, and subscribe to *Hello! Canada*, a Canadian magazine weirdly fixated on the lives of minor members of the British royal family.

Okay, maybe they are idiots just a little bit.

Monarchists are not idiots. There is no better place in the world than Canada to watch otherwise reasonable people prostrate themselves before a bunch of inbred European pricks. Margaret Atwood once admitted on Twitter that she is a monarchist. In 2009, prominent Canadian newspaper columnist Andrew Coyne argued that Canada should make Prince Harry the country's head of state.

He almost wore the same hat, which would have been awkward.

GETTING RID OF THE QUEEN

Few people care about whether Canada has a monarchy or not, least of all Canada's politicians. When asked whether he was considering abolition of the monarchy in 1998, Prime Minister Jean Chrétien said that he "already had enough trouble on [his] hands with the separatists of Québec." Pierre Trudeau: "I wouldn't lift a finger to get rid of the monarchy." Former Governor General Ed Schreyer said that "on a list of 100 things that need fixing, the monarchy ranks 101st."

INFOBOX

The Canadian Criminal Code stipulates that a judge, mayor, sheriff, or prison warden, upon being informed of a riot, must go to the riot and proclaim:

"Her Majesty the Queen charges and commands all persons being assembled immediately to disperse and peaceably to depart to their habitations or to their lawful business on the pain of being guilty of an offence for which, on conviction, they may be sentenced to imprisonment for life. GOD SAVE THE QUEEN."

This is the speech that finally ended the 2011 Vancouver riots.

These people are all promising an old British woman that they will do anything she or her shitty children tell them to do.

SO YOU WANT TO MOVE TO CANADA!

Fed up with your own democracy or war-torn hellhole and ready to make good on your threat to move to Canada? Why not load up the minivan and get waved through the border by smiling Mounties? After that, it's a free colonoscopy or two before starting a new life in Dildo, Newfoundland. But not so fast! Immigration, Refugees and Citizenship Canada wants to ensure that if you emigrate to Canada the process will be as annoying and invasive as possible.

INFOBOX

Canadian Oath of Citizenship: "I swear (or affirm) that I will be faithful and bear true allegiance to Her Majesty Queen Elizabeth the Second, Queen of Canada, Her Heirs and Successors, and that I will faithfully observe the laws of Canada and fulfil my duties as a Canadian citizen."

An ad for Halifax's Immigration Settlement and Integration Services, since renamed the Departmental Agency of Emigrant Settlement and Hospitality.

HOW TO BECOME A CANADIAN CITIZEN

A SIMPLE GUIDE (TO HOW DIFFICULT IT WILL BE)

1. Canada lets in around 680 immigrants daily (248,000 per year). Each has to first apply to become a permanent resident through one of several streams: family, economic, refugee, pouty American, etc.

2. Each stream has its own requirements, but the important thing to remember is that after months spent filling out forms, conducting interviews, getting physicals, and paying thousands of dollars in fees, you probably will still be arbitrarily rejected.

The ideal Canadian citizen is someone who will cheerfully put up with years of bureaucratic probing and thousands of pages of forms without complaining.

3. If you like unemployment, try the Federal Skilled Workers, Federal Skilled Trades, or Canada Experience Class programs. If you're useful (an engineer or a doctor), you might have a chance. Once you're in our glorious country, your credentials are no good, but you can join the ranks of taxi drivers who are qualified but not allowed to build dams or reattach retinas.

4. If you thought your minimalist graphic design style and love of Montréal indie rock would get you in, you are shit out of luck. The easiest way in is to get a job here and prove to the government that no Canadian is qualified to fill it. If your chosen profession is "bitterly underemployed cartoonist/drone-rock loopmaker," we are full up.

This is all slightly easier if you're fleeing genocide or something.

5. Sucker a Canadian into marrying you and apply for Spouse or Common Law Partner in Canada status. This lets you bypass the job requirement part, provided you can prove your love to the government. "Love" means sending government officials hundreds of pages of personal documents and photos to prove your romance is true. After filling out a stack of forms, you will be prodded by an Immigration Canada–approved doctor who will determine if you are medically capable of being loved. This costs only $200.

6. While you wait for your permanent residency to be processed, you can't work, so please arrive wealthy. You will need to prove your proficiency in both official languages. Expected wait time: 4 to 110+ months.

A wealthy person? Oh, hello, wealthy person! Yes, please come right this way. No, no, forget about those stupid forms. What's that behind your ear? Why, look, it's your Canadian citizenship certificate!

7. After somewhere between six months and eight years, you will receive a letter from the Canadian government saying that you will soon get another letter saying whether you were accepted.

8. Four to six weeks later, a letter will inform you that you have achieved permanent residency! (Or not.) Congratulations! Now, it's only five more years of waiting until you can apply to be a citizen, at which point you have to do the whole process over again.

THE DIFFERENCE BETWEEN PERMANENT RESIDENCY AND CITIZENSHIP

Permanent Residency	Citizenship
You must reside within the country for at least two years within a five-year period.	Travel, move somewhere else, burn a flag. Who cares?
You can't vote! So don't.	You can vote! But won't.
Your PR card must be renewed every five years.	You can get a Canadian passport! Your movements will now be tracked by an RFID chip and reported to partner countries, like the one you have fled.
You can be deported if you do something that freaks out the Canadian government, like conspire to commit terrorist acts or deface statues of Ted Rogers.	Under Bill C-24, you can be stripped of your citizenship without trial. After heavily criticizing the bill as a candidate, Prime Minister Justin Trudeau revoked more Canadian passports than his predecessor, who introduced the bill.

For a shameful period in the early twentieth century, Canada restricted Asian immigration with the Chinese head tax, the Korean torso tax, and the Japanese neck tax.

TRICKING PEOPLE INTO MOVING HERE

"Everything will be better in Winnipeg," said a surprising number of people.

anada has not always been a destination country. For most of its history, the only way to convince anyone to move here was by lying to them about how great Canada is.

LIES WE'VE TOLD IMMIGRANTS

Nineteeth-century immigration officials were instructed to laugh and change the subject whenever newcomers asked why the prairies were so empty.

IT'S NOT COLD, IT'S INVIGORATING

Before photography and the Internet, official immigration material was forbidden from mentioning the weather. The word "snow" was never used. "Cold" was replaced with words like "invigorating" and "bracing." Canada's climate was referred to as "the healthiest in the world."

EVERYONE TOTALLY WANTS TO LIVE HERE

Over half the original British colonists who came to Canada in the nineteenth century left for the United States within a few decades. In the early twentieth century, Ukrainian immigrants in Alberta would spend the first day on their new homesteads crying. Others reportedly shot themselves. For decades, migration away from Canada was just as high as immigration.

This Swedish settler hanged herself eight hours after posing for this advertisement.

THIS IS A UNIFORMLY DESIRABLE PLACE TO LIVE

After World War II, thousands of imported German POWs in Canada (many of them teenagers) said they wanted to stay here. Searching for opportunity, they took trains to nearly empty northern prairie towns where no one would ask what they'd been doing before 1945.

Immigrants were also lured with unrealistically cheery settlement names. Saskatchewan still has eighteen towns and incorporated areas named Constant Oral.

IF YOU MOVE HERE, YOU WON'T WANT TO KILL YOURSELF

Immigrant groups have their own sayings about how much they regret moving to Canada. Russians: "The mosquitoes suck more Russian blood than the landlords ever did in the old country." Italians: "I was told the roads here would be paved in gold. It turned out the roads weren't even paved and that I was expected to pave them." Poles: "I was told that Canada smelled of tree sap. But really it smells of hard labor."

WELCOME TO CANADA! (YOU GOT PLAYED)

In the early nineteenth century, Britain coaxed hundreds of thousands of people into moving to Canada with promises of rustic log cabin living, growing their own food, and no taxes. British immigrants quickly realized they'd been had. Building a log cabin wasn't nearly as easy as everyone thought, and most new immigrants became disenchanted with the New World. Susanna Moodie, one of Canada's first-known travel writers and best-known complainers, famously said that "the longer you remain in Canada, the less you like it." Many early immigrants eventually moved to the States.

How hard is your life if building a log cabin is easy?

To this day, Canada continues its proud tradition of deception. Our universities and colleges spend millions convincing high school kids from all over the world to come to Canada for a world-class post-secondary education. Once they get here, these foreign students learn they're attending professional colleges with no student housing, exorbitant international tuition rates, and lecture halls packed to capacity.

Fortunately, most students immediately become too high to notice.

Workers from countries like Mexico and the Philippines are promised gainful employment and a path to permanent residence through initiatives such as the Temporary Foreign Worker Program and the Seasonal Agricultural Worker Program. When workers arrive here, they often find sub-minimum-wage work, zero social safety net, no protection from abusive employers, and Tim Hortons customers who throw tantrums if their bagels aren't toasted in a very specific way.

Due to an immigration policy that functioned on the same rules as sitcom casting, every rural Canadian town was given precisely one Chinese family in the 1950s.

WE EVEN LIED TO RICH WHITE PEOPLE

No one is safe from Canadian tourism spin, not even wealthy literate Americans. Over the last seventy years, Canada has placed hundreds of ads in the *New Yorker* trying to convince the magazine's readers that Canada is a welcoming, highly advanced country. Here are some excerpts:

 You will enjoy every day of exhilarating sunshine."

—June 1, 1935

 Come for a weekend or come for a month. Come whichever way suits you best—by road, air or rail. Whatever kind of vacation you want, at whatever price."

Just come. Please. It'll be good, we swear.

—February 14, 1977

 Smile, you're in Canada. Enjoy the out-of-doors and gape at one of the true wonders of the world. Squeal as snow goes down your back because laughter is in our nature."

Also in our nature: hypothermia, death from frostbite, bears.

—January 14, 2002

 Imagine yourself standing in a place where no human sound touches your ear, the leafless trees allow you to gaze farther than you thought possible and, for miles, the only neighbors you find are sporting feathers and fur. If you feel goosebumps riding up your arms, don't worry, it's natural."

The only human sound you'll hear is your own soul screaming.

—October 14, 2002

This ship's entire crew died months before the ship got stuck on ice.

CANADA: NOT BY CHOICE

Canada is kinda hard to miss, and the men who "discovered" it were not a bunch of geniuses. European explorers found Canada reluctantly, by accident, and did a messy job of it.

Vikings actually found Canada first. Unfortunately for the modern jellied-egg industry, Canada was quickly abandoned as a Scandinavian colony.

THE VOYAGES OF CANADA'S REALLY GARBAGE FIRST EXPLORERS

CABOT'S FIRST VOYAGE Left immediately, didn't even set foot on land.

CABOT'S SECOND VOYAGE Walked about fifteen meters, got scared, turned back.

CARTIER'S FIRST VOYAGE   Kidnapped a young Iroquois boy just 'cause.

CARTIER'S SECOND VOYAGE   Returned to kidnap the rest of the young boy's family.

HUDSON'S FINAL VOYAGE   Set adrift by mutineers.

CHAMPLAIN'S EXPLORATION OF QUÉBEC   Shot two Iroquois chiefs, sparking a century of terrible French-Iroquois relations.

Jacques Cartier called his North American discovery "New France," which is still 400 percent more creative than "Newfoundland."

"Oh, you found Québec, how quaint. I got bored between discovering Australia and Hawaii, so I decided to discover British Columbia."
—Captain James Cook

WHAT DO YOU MEAN THIS ISN'T CHINA?

Most early explorers arrived in Canada by accident on their way to plunder the Far East. John Cabot, on a mission to find a route to China, was so disappointed with his discovery of Canada that he didn't even bother getting off the boat the first time around. He returned a year later, but didn't explore "beyond the shooting distance of a crossbow." He remained just long enough to claim the land for England and pronounce the whole area Catholic. So, about fifteen minutes.

According to their respective statues in Canadian cities, these explorers spent most of their time covered in bird shit and pointing confidently into the distance.

Soon, word spread across Europe that there was a large land mass sitting between Europe and China, so explorers desperately started looking for a way around it. The hunt for the then-hypothetical Northwest Passage was all the rage, so England kept throwing ill-equipped explorers at the Arctic, perhaps in hopes that their frozen corpses would form a solid mass people could walk across.

ALL ABOARD THE HMS *TERROR*

John Franklin wasn't the British navy's first choice to lead a dangerous expedition to the Arctic. He was their sixth choice, so, naturally, he is one of Canada's best-known explorers. His first two Canadian voyages had gone well since he'd come back and all, so when he was at the virile age of fifty-nine, the British gave Franklin command of two ships. Aboard the aptly named HMS *Terror* and *Erebus*, Franklin and his crew voyaged to the New World, only to be thoroughly bitch-slapped by the weather. In their failed attempts to chart the Arctic, Franklin and his men tried to survive by eating moss, their boots, and, finally, each other.

Moss, boots, and human flesh were still tastier than most white people foods at the time.

Franklin's last recorded diary entry was: "It sure would be nice if we could get rid of this ice with some sort of irreversible man-made shift in global temperatures."

WHAT DO WE DO WITH TWO FROZEN BOATS?

After the disappearance of Franklin's expedition, his wife sponsored seven fruitless searches in over twenty-five years to determine the location of the *Erebus* and the *Terror,* proving that good dick was hard to find in Victorian England. The mystery of the Franklin Expedition's fate has resulted in many attempts to find the ships. Naval researchers, historians, and archaeologists have devoted decades to the quest, hoping global warming would hurry up so they could search the ice. In 2014, the *Erebus* was found in the Queen Maud Gulf. In 2016, the *Terror* was found just inside Terror Bay (!), the spot where Indigenous people had rumored it to be but had kept it to themselves for a laugh.

For many Inuit, starving, wild-eyed cannibals from the Franklin Expedition were the first white men they saw.

WELCOME TO INDIAN RESERVES! BRING YOUR OWN ~~WATER~~ EVERYTHING

Today, reserves are choice pieces of land in the most hidden corners of Canada where Indigenous people can live and grow ever more resentful of Canada's ongoing Trudeau obsession. While mired in poor social and economic conditions, First Nations people remain proudly connected to their reserves and land. Reserves are enclaves where Indigenous Canadians can freely practice their cultures, speak their languages, and maintain their unique identities.

HISTORY

In their colonization of Canada, the Fathers of Confederation graciously embraced their roles as evil stepfathers to these troublesome Indigenous children. While extremely good at helping colonists survive in Canada's climate or at fighting against American revolutionaries, the Indigenous people kept annoyingly insisting they had rights to the land they'd lived on for centuries. So the new Canadian government wrote the Indian Act, which gave themselves control over Indian status, Indian governments, and the management of Indian lands, called "reserves." They even started calling them "Indians."

Canada aimed to eradicate "Indian" culture and to assimilate them into the body politic by segregating Indians onto small, isolated tracts of reserve land spread out across Canada's more undesirable areas. Residents had to get passes to leave the reserves, a new governance structure was imposed called the "band council system," and individual ownership of reserve land was prohibited.

WHERE TO GO

Canada has over 630 exciting First Nations reserves to visit! Their populations range anywhere from 100 to 20,000 registered souls. Gone are the days of tepees and horse riding. These traditions have been replaced with dilapidated, moldy houses, free-range rez dogs, and deafening silence.

Each reserve has its own distinct people, culture, language, and hockey team. To visit the more remote reserves, prepare to pay upward of $2,000. Stay long enough and you can catch a free flight home during the annual flooding evacuations.

WHAT TO SEE

CIGARETTE SHACKS

Smoke shops line the streets/single unpaved road, offering customers cheap cartons of cigarettes and the joy of knowing they are supporting Indigenous economic development.

BAND OFFICE

Meet the elected chief and council, sometimes made up of one prominent family on the reserve. Band elections are held every two years, so be nice to the lady who runs the cigarette shack. Her mom is running for chief next year.

CASINOS AND BINGO HALLS

Some of the last places in Canada where you can smoke freely indoors while emptying your wallets chasing "G53."

SACRED TREE

Visit Seine River First Nation's oldest and most sacred tree: Grandfather Running Sap. He's seen the wars between the

Anishnawbe and the bloodthirsty Crees, the expansion of Hudson's Bay Canada, and the installation of band wifi, all while throwing shade at the Canadian Shield.

WHAT TO BRING

WATER Bring your own drinkable water because at any given time there will be over 130 drinking-water advisories at over 80 reserves.

FOOD Reserves aren't usually culinary hot spots, but, as in any fancy eatery, you should prepare to pay $13 for a bag of apples or $33 for a bag of flour in the most remote communities.

A GOVERNMENT OFFICIAL If you're visiting, be sure to come with a member of the federal government so that the trip will be properly documented by media. Why take your own photos when the press will do it for you?

INFOBOX

Canada's Indian Act and reserve system helped inspire the South African government's apartheid policy.

Little-known fact: the White House was actually designed to be constantly on fire.

THE BIRTH OF CANADIAN HUMBLE SUPERIORITY

C an you smell that? The faint stench of pretension that fills the air whenever a Canadian talks about the United States or the wider world? That's Canadian humble superiority, and it's been lingering ever since 1812, when the Canadians deluded themselves into thinking they had won a war against the Americans.

How bad does your war have to be to not even get a real name?

Of course, this is a fairy tale. The War of 1812 was the biggest non-event in Canadian history, determined by a series of stupid mistakes. It had no cool or memorable battles, resulted in no changes to national boundaries, and ended in a tie.

WE'D CALL OFF THE WAR, BUT THAT WOULD BE AWKWARD

The War of 1812, also known as the War of Faulty Communication, did not need to happen. The Americans declared war on the Brits/Canadians without knowing that their major grievance (trade restrictions) had been rectified three weeks prior. Since it took news three weeks to cross the ocean, they decided to just go ahead with the war anyway, because the only thing more embarrassing than calling off a wedding is calling off a war.

Guns at that time didn't work when it rained, so all the War of 1812's major battles had to take place in sunny weather, which was nice.

"YOU'RE NOT MY DAD!"

The United States had some unresolved daddy issues with England. Looking to offload their country's impotent rage, President Madison decided Canada was a perfect target: annexed British territory would add to America's landmass while also sticking it to those tea-drinking bastards. The British, though, were stuck in the Napoleonic Wars, so they figured they'd let the colonies sort it out themselves. It was a win-win for the USA. Until the Napoleonic Wars ended and the British sent their army to burn down every building that mattered to the Americans.

WE BURNED THE WHITE HOUSE UNTIL IT WAS BLACK

Canada's proudest moment was helping the Brits torch the White House, the Capitol building, and the US Treasury Building to retaliate for the burning of Port Dover and York (now Toronto). One of the less-proud moments was when Canadian and British soldiers had to pile up furniture as kindling because the well-constructed stone White House wouldn't catch fire.

Military historians generally agree that getting your capital burned down means that you probably didn't win a war.

EVERYONE'S A WINNER! OR A LOSER! (BUT THAT POV IS BAD FOR MORALE!)

The Americans probably would have given up northern Maine in the Treaty of Ghent if the British had asked, but they forgot.

Ask an American who won the war, they'll say the States. Ask a Canadian, and we'll say we crushed them. After a suitable number of people were killed on both sides, the war ended in the lamest military stalemate ever: the Treaty of Ghent. Even the name sounds like an ambivalent grunt.

Despite the anticlimactic shrug of a resolution, both countries still look back on the war as a great moment in their fetal periods of statehood. Accounts of the war have taken on a fairy-tale quality, and most forget that boundaries remained completely unchanged after tens of thousands of needless deaths. Victory for everyone!

CANADA & THE US: FROM ENEMIES TO BESTIES

The War of 1812 is officially the last interesting thing that happened to the Niagara Peninsula.

For Canada it was the era of "holy shit we might actually have to fortify this place."

The most notable thing to come out of the war was Canada's newfound self-congratulatory confidence, gained by defending itself from a largely incompetent army. We haven't stopped patting ourselves on the back for that one. The end of the war almost immediately brought on a period dubbed the "era of good feelings" and led to unrestricted trade between the United States and Canada, although ultimately we knew we were better than them. So everything was hunky-dory. (Minus the many Indigenous people who were killed and had their land forcibly taken. But it was inconvenient for anyone to acknowledge that. What, it still is? Huh.)

POP QUIZ!

LAURA SECORD IS

A. An 1812 war heroine

B. A duplicitous snitch

C. Some chocolate lady, I don't know

D. All of the above

Answer: D

This is the only portrait of Laura Secord, one of the most famous women in Canadian history. Except it is actually a painting of some elder statesman, with the beard removed, and a bonnet painted over.

This general is dying from how unsatisfying and low-stakes the War of 1812 was.

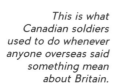

This is what Canadian soldiers used to do whenever anyone overseas said something mean about Britain.

STILLBIRTH OF A NATION

C anada pulled its weight during World Wars I and II and is widely believed to have "come into its own" on the global stage as a result. In truth, we had little choice but to participate, and our involvement as the Allies' proudest meat-shield was more a statement of our dependence than of our independence.

INFO**BOX**

John McCrae's "In Flanders Fields," a famous poem memorializing Canada's war dead that we make every child in grade school learn by heart, was first published in *Punch*, a British humor and satire magazine. People still don't get the joke.

WORLD WAR I

"IF YOU SAY SO, PART I"

At the start of World War I, Canada was still a British Dominion, so, by law, we had to join the war when we were told to. The 1914 War Measures Act gave sweeping powers to the ruling government in the name of national safety. A large portion of the Act was dedicated to rounding up and imprisoning "enemy aliens," including new Canadians from Ukraine, Germany, and Austria-Hungary, many of whom had already fled persecution in their own countries. Berlin, Ontario, was scared shitless and changed its name to Kitchener.

Banff and Jasper National Parks were built, in part, by interned Germans. If "building stuff with forced labor" wasn't a touchy issue for Germans, they'd probably bring this up more often.

ONLY WHITES CAN FIGHT, UNTIL THEY GET DESPERATE

At first, only white soldiers had the honor of being killed by Germans. Indigenous soldiers were resentfully tolerated, and Black Acadians who offered their service were refused entrance into this "white man's war." After much death, the army had a progressive epiphany and decided that minorities could die, too.

CANADIANS YPRES'D IN THEIR HANKIES TO SURVIVE

At the Battle of Ypres, Canadian soldiers were among the first to suffer chlorine gas attacks. They peed into handkerchiefs; the ammonia in urine neutralized the active compounds in the gas. This guaranteed that fourteen-year-olds would remember at least one fact from history class.

Many Canadian map features were named in the fervor of WWI, like Vimy, Alberta; Victory Mountain, and Disembowel Anyone Who Looks like the Kaiser Lookout.

CANADA'S "BIRTH OF A NATION"

Brigadier-General Alexander Ross said he witnessed "the birth of a nation" at Vimy Ridge. It was the first time the Canadian Corps fought on their own and they did so by throwing their bodies and shrapnel at a German-controlled hill called "the Pimple" until it popped.

WORLD WAR II

"IF YOU SAY SO, PART II"

The Allies had to politely turn down Canada's offer to build Nazi-proof aircraft carriers out of ice.

Canada declared war on Germany in 1939, two years before the United States, which is pretty badass. To get there, Canada asked King George VI for permission to declare war, which is less badass.

In truth, the request was a formality. We were always going to follow Britain into war, but we waited a week so it seemed like it was our idea.

"IF DAY"

To get Canadians super-stoked about the war, the government terrorized its own citizens with a prank invasion, dubbed "If Day." In partnership with the Greater Winnipeg Victory Loan Company, the Canadian Forces staged a German invasion of Winnipeg in 1942 to "bring the war home." Actors in Nazi uniforms harassed citizens and simulated a firefight against real Canadian forces with fake bombings and threats of internment. Horrified citizens bought war bonds in droves, so the stunt was both successful and insane, somehow convincing people that Winnipeg was worth invading.

Classic Nazi humor included jokes like:

Q: "Who was that lady I saw you out with last night?"

A: "That was my wife!"

(Respondent is required to laugh.)

The *Winnipeg Free Press* also joined in with spreads that included jokes the Nazis might make. More than anything, the Canadian government wanted to show their people the scary world of German humor.

CANADA ON JEWS: "NONE IS TOO MANY"

Canada's wartime government turned away most Jews fleeing Europe from 1930 to 1939. In 1939, more than 900 refugees on the MS *St. Louis* were rejected before they reached Halifax and sent back to Europe, where many were captured and killed by Germans.

The fake Germans burned preselected books in front of the Winnipeg Public Library, still a great solution for dealing with Winnipeg weather in February.

In Canada, some German Jews were sent to internment camps alongside Nazi-sympathizing Germans, because the government couldn't tell the difference. As a result, today's fully integrated Jewish Canadians keep a little "Fuck you, Canada" stored away.

THERE MUST BE A BETTER WAY TO "FORGE"

Canadians "forged their identity" again through copious bloodshed on the beaches of Normandy. Canadians were primarily deployed to Juno Beach, which was initially code-named Jelly, but was changed because it was apparently too silly a name for a place where hundreds of men would be brutally destroyed by industrialized weaponry. Of the five beach assaults comprising D-Day, the assault at Juno was the most successful. The Juno Beach assault would probably be more famous but the Canadians unfortunately came from the D-Day country with the worst filmmakers.

If not for WWII, you'd have to find somewhere else to drink other than the Legion, you ungrateful hipster bastard.

SEPARATIST MOVEMENTS

I f you've ever been in Canada and felt an overwhelming urge to get the fuck out, you're not alone. Almost every part of Canada has tried to leave. Here's what it would look like if they were all successful.

THE YUKON AND NORTHWEST TERRITORIES

Not a real separatist movement, but already pretty much separate from Canada in most of the meaningful ways.

BIOREGION OF CASCADIA

Too beautiful, progressive, wealthy, and resource-rich to slum it with the rest of the United States and Canada. When we need to pick people to send to Mars to restart civilization, the residents of Cascadia will be the obvious choice.

In their words: Regions should be based on their interconnected ecosystems rather than arbitrary political boundaries. Also, no uglies allowed.

Why it failed: Took shrooms and forgot.

THE REPUBLIC OF WESTERN CANADA

White people who favor looser gun legislation, drive trucks, and think they're cowboys are a distinct and special culture not found anywhere else in the world, and they deserve their own country.

In their words: We are NOT in this together.

Why it failed: After the price of oil dropped, realized that, you know what, we are in this together.

THE AUTONOMOUS REGIONS OF NUNAVUT, NUNAVIK AND NUNATSIAVUT

It's not separating since we were here first.

In their words: We survived colonialism and we will survive you.

NEW NEWFOUNDLAND AND LABRADOR

Newfoundland and Labrador didn't even join Confederation until 1949. So this isn't so much a separation as the cancellation of a subscription after a trial period.

Why it failed: The same general lack of judgment and foresight that led it to join in the first place.

MARITIME UNION

Rooted in the strong suspicion that the federal government may have forgotten they exist.

Emancipation strategy: Try to get picked up by the US as a bundled package. Maybe throw in Newfoundland and Labrador to sweeten the deal.

LA RÉPUBLIQUE DU QUÉBEC

Crisse! Vous comprenez toujours pas pourquoi? Permettez-moi de vous expliquer encore une fois, en termes simples:

"Le Canada, ce n'est pas mon pays. Le Québec y est." Point final.

In their words: Distinct culture, distinct smell, infrastructure that is crumbling in a distinctly Francophone way.

Why it failed: Only in the minds of naïve Anglophones.

THE PROVINCE OF TORONTO

"To secure more power, autonomy, and clout" for the city of Toronto.

In their words: We are just one Japanese cheesecake store away from being New York.

THE PROVINCE OF NORTHERN ONTARIO

A century of financial mismanagement left it with an eighteenth-century economy.

In their words: We need more manufacturing jobs, fighting belongs in hockey, no gays allowed.

QUÉBEC: DISTINCTLY DISTINCT DISTINCTNESS

Québec is the sullen teenager in the happy Canadian family. Québec wants you to know that she's not like you, you don't understand her, she hasn't forgotten all the shit you put her through, and she'll be much happier when she moves out. But for now she wants more money for hanging out and fucking around. You'd better give it to her, or she will make your life truly miserable.

As most Québecers descended from only 10,000 original French settlers, many have unwittingly slept with a cousin. A sexy, sexy cousin.

INFO**BOX**

Québec claims that it is very, very "secular." But did you know that there is a massive crucifix hanging in the Québec legislature? Or that there is a giant cross on top of the mountain overlooking Montréal? Did you know that Québec is completely covered in crosses? Except this is fine, because they are a part of Québec's "cultural heritage!"

VIVE LE QUÉBEC LIBRE

The Québécois do have a legitimate beef. They went from being the castoffs of France to the vassals of Britain to the ridiculed stepchildren of dull Protestant English Canada. All the while, they were kept dirt poor and knocked-up by the Catholic Church.

Through it all, they developed and held on to an ancient dialect, a genuinely, deliciously unhealthy cuisine, and a charming "eh, fuck it!" attitude. Add to all that a seething anger, and you get a political movement in the late 1960s called the Quiet Revolution, which was clearly not named by anyone who has been cornered by a French separatist in a Québec pub.

During Québec's more authoritarian, Catholic past, the Just for Laughs festival was known as the Feel Guilty About Pooping Festival.

After Northern Ireland, Québec is home to the world's largest population of former terrorists who are now bitter, sweater-wearing Internet commenters.

THE PLIGHT OF DISTINCTION

In the 1960s, Québec premier Jean Lesage coined the term "distinct society" to describe his province. Ever since, the whole country has been fighting about what that means exactly. Those who claim Québec is a "distinct society" want it to be formally recognized in the Constitution, because it wouldn't hurt Canada to say something nice once in a while.

WHAT MAKES IT SO DISTINCT?

RAMPANT CORRUPTION

High-ranking politicians are charged and arrested for their links to organized crime. Mayors regularly resign over corruption allegations. The construction industry is plagued by Mafia ties as well as shoddy workmanship. Québec launched a multimillion-dollar commission in 2011 to figure out why Québec politics is so corrupt. Their solution? Arrest everyone.

DREAMS OF RACIAL PURITY

Who said the disastrous ethno-nationalism of the early twentieth century has gone out of style? Québec identity rests on the poorly maintained intersection of ethnicity and linguistics. They even have a word for "pure" Québécers who can trace their ancestry back to the original settlers of New France without any gross fraternization with the Scots or the English. If you can prove this, congratulations! You are a *pure laine* Québecois. It literally means "pure wool." You're the best of the sheep.

FASCIST SECULARISM

When Québecers dropped religion, they dropped it hard. They kicked it, spat on it, and made every church in Montréal into a condo. Taking a page from their deadbeat dad, France, they then started looking for other religions to kick around.

Québec parents are least likely to cry when their children decide to pursue a career as a human statue.

In 2013, just before the separatist Parti Québécois called for an election that they would ultimately lose by a humiliating margin, they proposed the Values Charter. It would have restricted public sector employees from wearing any outwardly religious symbols. Turbans, kippahs, and hijabs would have been a no-go. Initially, support for the charter actually outweighed the opposition. Because values.

ANCIENT FRENCH SWEARING

After the French Revolution, the dominant dialect of France was that of the bourgeois class. Across the Atlantic, Québec retained its older French dialect. In a nod to its religious roots, Québec's cuss words are all about flipping off the church: *Tabarnak!* (tabernacle) and *câlisse!* (chalice) are considered filthier versions of "fuck."

THE LANGUAGE POLICE

The province has a law enforcement agency with the power to punish speakers of English and other non-French languages. They investigate cereal boxes, dismantle street signs and issue fines to ethnic restaurants for punctuation that looks too English. Here are a few of their greatest hits.

BEEF CLOWN WON'T BACK DOWN (1977)

After the language laws were enacted, McDonald's was told to comply with French punctuation and remove its apostrophe from all signage. The burger chain threatened to pack up their special sauce and leave the province before they'd bastardize their brand. After a tense standoff, the language cops granted McDonald's a rare concession.

The sovereignty movement has yet to recover from this.

NOODLEGATE (2013)

An inspector from the Québec Board of the French Language demanded that an Italian restaurant remove the foreign term "pasta" from its menu.

FRENCHBOOK (2014)

A women's clothing store owner was directed to translate her store's Facebook page to French or face legal consequences.

50 percent of Quebec's post-referendum concession speeches have been delivered drunk.

NECESSARY CENSORSHIP (2014)

American retailers, including Pottery Barn, were forced to geo-block their websites from Québec users because they were not in French. Even four thousand uses of the word *chaise* were deemed insufficient.

THE PEOPLE WHO RUN CANADA

OUR FACELESS OVERLORDS

For all we know, these people could literally have no faces. Their faces could just be smooth expanses of skin and we wouldn't know.

Billionaires in other countries often do tacky and attention-seeking things like running for president or giving their fortunes to charity. Not in Canada. Here, a handful of super-rich families have the good sense to lie low and avoid publicity while they enjoy some of the world's lowest corporate tax rates. And thanks to the complete absence of inheritance or estate taxes in Canada, they can keep their wealth locked within their private clans forever, regardless of how shitty their offspring might turn out to be.

Canada's robber barons have few hospitals, museums, galleries or universities to their names. Most of them don't even live here. And most Canadians don't know they exist.

THE THOMSONS

NET WORTH $39 billion (richest family in Canada).

GOT RICH Buying radio stations and newspapers, immediately firing people to increase profits, which they then used to borrow more money. Ideologically indifferent, the Thomsons bought right-wing and communist papers around the world. Once owned three hundred newspapers in Africa.

GOT SUPER-RICH Bringing commercial TV to the UK. Paid peanuts for rights to shows like *Gilligan's Island*, generating monstrous profits without creating any original programming. Roy Thomson's broadcast license inspired him to coin the phrase "a licence to print money."

He proceeded to make a fortune licensing T-shirt rights to this phrase.

STAY RICH Through epic frugality. Kenneth Thomson, when already a millionaire scion, carried his books to private school in paper bags. He later showed up to meetings with holes in his shoes and paid surprise visits to companies he had acquired, to turn off their air conditioning.

Kenneth preferred that employees simply call him Ken, to save money.

MEDIA STRATEGY Owning the media. The Thomsons have a controlling interest in the *Globe and Mail* and in the Thomson Reuters newswire.

GIVING BACK   Ken Thomson owned a large collection of bad paintings by Cornelius Krieghoff, most of which depict snow. He hung these on the walls of the Thomsons corporate headquarters and had the place designated a public art gallery for tax purposes. The public was not informed.

THE IRVINGS

NET WORTH $7.6 billion.

GOT RICH   Selling oil and buying trees.

GOT SUPER-RICH   Buying more trees. The Irvings own more land than any other person on the planet who is not royalty or a pope. Sadly, most of it is in New Brunswick and Maine.

STAY RICH   By strong-arming government into unprecedented tax breaks. They employ one in ten people in New Brunswick and constantly threaten to leave the province. As a result, they pay less property tax on their gas depot than a nearby hospital does.

Which is weird given the fact that they probably own the hospital, too.

MEDIA STRATEGY   Owning the media. Their local media monopoly caused the federal government to declare New Brunswick "a journalistic disaster zone." The Irvings' newspapers avoid covering the Irvings, and rival news sources are quickly undercut and/or purchased.

GIVING BACK   The Irving family is known to be secretive when it comes to its philanthropy. The secret is either that they are very humble about their philanthropy or that they don't do much of it.

NOT AT ALL CREEPY   Patriarch K. C. Irving died in New Brunswick but was buried next to his wife in his tax haven, Bermuda. Later, they were both exhumed and reburied in New Brunswick on the Irving manor in graves marked only "Grammy and Grampy."

"Grammy and Grampy" is also what the citizens of New Brunswick are required to call members of the Irving family.

"Jimmy Pattison" That sounds made-up, right? That's because Jimmy Pattison is essentially a cartoon business person. Close your eyes and imagine a self-made billionaire person named "Jimmy Pattison." That's pretty much Jimmy Pattison.

JIMMY PATTISON

NET WORTH $5.7 billion (Canada's richest person).

GOT RICH   Selling used cars.

GOT SUPER-RICH   Selling more used cars. Got into food and media. GE CEO Jack Welch's famous habit of automatically firing the bottom 10 percent of his staff every year is rumored to have been inspired by Pattison.

MEDIA STRATEGY   Owning the media. The Jim Pattison Group is "Canada's largest private western-based radio and television company."

GIVING BACK   Pattison is a devout Christian who reportedly funds an "ecstatic" evangelical school that gives enrolment priority to students who have spoken in tongues. His company also distributes porn.

NOT AT ALL CREEPY   Owns world's largest collection of shrunken heads. They're owned by a small subsidiary of his company, Ripley's Believe It or Not!, which is run by his son Jim Jr.

SUCCESSION   Pattison is eighty-seven years old and has not disclosed a successor. Son Jim Jr. is himself "nearing a conventional retirement age."

THE SAPUTOS

NET WORTH $10.6 billion.

GOT RICH   Through legitimate enterprises totally unrelated to an early business offer patriarch Giuseppe Saputo made to Joseph "Joe Bananas" Bonanno, boss of the Bonanno crime family.

GOT SUPER-RICH   With hard work and good fortune, and the 1972 police raid of the company yielded nothing.

STAYS RICH   "I can tell you," said Lino Saputo when questioned about rumored Mafia affiliations, "I've worked honestly all my life."

MEDIA STRATEGY   In 2008, Saputo Inc. sued a number of newspapers for falsely associating them with organized crime. An out-of-court settlement was reached in 2009, and a *La Presse* article was retracted.

There has never been any contact between Giuseppe Saputo and Joe Bananas, boss of one of the Five Families.

FOREIGN POLICY

anada is a joiner. Whether you're the USA, Britain, or heck, even the USA, Canada can usually be counted on to ride along on your fun adventures in faraway lands. It's cool to have big, powerful friends, and we can be counted on to chip in for gas or whip out a few CF-18s whenever those friends decide to uphold colonialism, appease a dictator, or bumble backward into some ill-conceived military escapade in the Levant. If you're looking for a coalition, consider us willing!

Other activities we would like in on: craft beer tastings, corporate retreats, anything with free food.

A HISTORY OF GOING WITH THE FLOW

AGREE-TO-WHAT-THE-BIG-KIDS-WANT DIPLOMACY

Canada is like that obnoxious kid who sucked up to all the bullies at your high school.

In the 1903 Alaska Boundary Dispute, the British pretended to care about the random lines Canada wanted drawn on a map. A panel of three Americans, two Canadians, and one Brit decided that America should get more of Alaska; the vote against Canada came from the British judge. Canada decided to go along with it. In 1909, the Governor General and the British ambassador to the US both asked Prime Minister Wilfrid Laurier to create a separate department to manage Canada's squabbles with the United States.

MOMMY IS ALWAYS RIGHT

As war with Germany looked imminent for Britain in 1914, Canada looked at its tiny military and handful of ships and said, "Oh yeah, we want in on that." Three days before Britain declared war, the Canadians sent the British government a telegram assuring they would join the war, to which the British responded, "Well, duh!" The story is the same for pretty much every other large-scale military adventure Canada has participated in since.

The British Foreign Office has mistakenly referred to every Canadian prime minister since 1960 as "Malcolm Diefenbaker." It is illegal to correct them.

In a 1985 telephone call about foreign affairs between Ronald Reagan and Brian Mulroney, the only recorded utterances from Mulroney were "Hell yeah!" and "You tell 'em, Gip!"

"PEACEKEEPING"

The peacekeeping soldiers in blue helmets are a Canadian invention. To keep the French, British, Israelis, Americans, and Egyptians from starting a conflict in the Middle East over the Suez Canal, Canada's foreign minister Lester B. Pearson suggested putting a couple thousand Canadians in everyone's way. For his diplomacy and ingenuity, he was awarded the Nobel Peace Prize and was later elected prime minister.

Canada's only meaningful contribution to the history of diplomacy is literally standing in the way and observing things.

Canada has only sort of dabbled in peacekeeping since. The country sent nine military observers to observe *something* in the UN mission to the Congo. In a stroke of efficiency Canada has sent fewer and fewer peacekeepers to global trouble spots while being more and more self-congratulating.

And nothing bad happened between Egypt and Israel ever again.

CAN WE HELP WITHOUT GETTING HURT?

We did not help invade Iraq, but we felt left out, so:

Canada also offered to build some kind of robotic arm to attach to the Iraq War, but was quietly rebuffed.

- three Canadian generals had combat roles in the invasion of Iraq.

- Canadian pilots and support crews helped coordinate air strikes.

- Canada's C-130s ferried US troops and weapons into Iraq.

We did not help invade Vietnam, but we realllly wanted to, so:

- 40,000 Canadian soldiers participated as volunteers.

- the Pentagon Papers revealed extensive Canadian involvement in military logistics.

- Agent Orange was tested in New Brunswick.

FANCY WAYS TO DESCRIBE STANDING IN THE MIDDLE

Canadian soldiers have been known to scratch the phrase "Neutral Helper Dudes" into the barrels of their guns and tattoo it across their chests.

Canada wants the world to think we are neutral helper dudes. Here is how we describe our role in foreign affairs:

BRIDGE BUILDER   University of Ottawa International Affairs professor Roland Paris: "Canada is not powerful enough to dictate to others, even if we wished to do so . . . We have succeeded in international affairs by building bridges, not burning them."

More suggestions: "Holder of Hands," "Bob the Builder," "Dancer Among Wolves," "Twirler of Skirt," "Fluffer."

HELPFUL FIXER   The *Economist*: "A country which rightly or wrongly loves to think of itself as being a 'helpful fixer' of the world's problems."

PROVIDER OF GOOD OFFICES   *Toronto Star* editorial: "Once universally welcomed as an honest broker, helpful fixer and provider of good offices . . ."

PEACEKEEPING SCORECARD

· Sassy blue helmets	+10
· Introduce cholera to post-earthquake Haiti	-75
· Kind of prevent massacre in Darfur	+30
· Prevent Cyprus from triggering World War III	+23
· Argo!	+10
· *Argo* the movie	-10
· Take fifty-five days to investigate a Canadian soldier who fathered a child while on a mission in crisis-stricken Haiti	-55
· Intervene only 20 percent of the time	+17
· Intervene only in countries ending in A the other 80 percent of the time (Bosnia, Rwanda, Kenya, Syria)	-80
· Allow Canadians to feel self-righteous	+130
GRAND TOTAL	**0**

ASJNFIJQPOKFMW MUCH?

Canada is an enthusiastic participator in the following international organizations: ADB, AfDB, APEC, ASEAN, BIS, CDB, EAPC, EBRD, FAO, FATF, G7, G8, G-10, G-20, IADB, IAEA, IBRD, ICAO, ICC, ICCt, ICRM, IDA, IEA, IFAD, IFC, IFRCS, IHO, ILO, IMF, IMO, IMSO, IOC, IOM, IPU, ISO, ITSO, ITU, ITUC, MIGA, MINUSTAH, MONUSCO, NAFTA, NATO, NEA, NSG, OAS, OECD, OIF, OPCW, OSCE, PCA, PIF, SECI, UN, UNAMID, UNCTAD, UNDOF, UNESCO, UNFICYP, UNHCR, UNMIS, UNRWA, UNWTO, UPU, WFTU, WHO, WIPO, WMO, WTO.

Canadians shipped overseas to fight in world wars were often so disoriented that they would literally lick the faces of their enemies.

LICK THEM *over there!*

COME ON CANADA !

NATIONAL DEFENSE

Asking a bunch of Canadian broskis what they would do if the US invaded is like throwing a ball of yarn into a room full of cats.

When it comes to security, you can pay for an expensive alarm system or you can put a sticker on your window saying that you did. Canada opts for the latter. Never have so few white people claimed a landmass so massive with such little effort. Canadians think that being invaded or conquered is so unlikely that for fun they routinely fantasize about being invaded—usually by the United States.

THE "TIN POT NAVY"

In 1910, war in Europe seemed imminent. Prime Minister Wilfrid Laurier came up with a plan for Canada's own navy, with warships for Canadians' use also available at Her Majesty's beck and call. Consisting of two former British Royal Navy ships, Laurier's "fleet" was dubbed the "tin pot navy" because it was a bunch of rusted junk. The plan angered French nationalists who didn't think Canada's navy should support Britain at all. English nationalists didn't think Canada's new navy could support Britain enough. It was another example of Laurier bridging the gap between French and English Canada by uniting them in contempt for him.

DEFENCE SCHEME NO. 1

The United States has had a few chances to invade and conquer Canada: the 1775 Continental Army's attack on Québec, the War of 1812, the Fenian raids, the *South Park* movie, and so on. But far from being some overripe fruit fit for Yankee plucking, Canada had her own designs on the States. Defence Scheme No. 1 was a surprise attack on the US cooked up in 1921 by Canadian military intelligence chief Brigadier General James "Buster" Sutherland Brown.

Officially, the Queen is the commander-in-chief of the Canadian Armed Forces.

Those were the good old days when conspiracy theorists actually acted on their beliefs.

Buster conducted five years of solo reconnaissance in preparation for the plan (map below). He traveled to rural cities in Vermont and North Dakota, snapped photos, collected local road maps from gas stations, and studied the peculiarities of his American targets.

Brown's idea lay dormant until 2003, when an online chat room set up by the Canadian Army revealed that soldiers frequently talked about when exactly they could expect the United States to invade and seize Canada's natural resources. The Canadians' best counter-plan? Burn the natural resources.

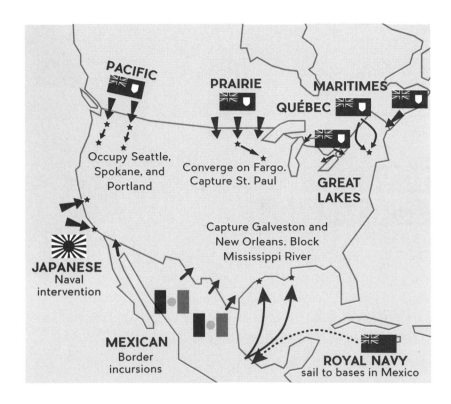

PACIFIC

PRAIRIE

MARITIMES

QUÉBEC

Occupy Seattle, Spokane, and Portland

Converge on Fargo. Capture St. Paul

GREAT LAKES

Capture Galveston and New Orleans. Block Mississippi River

JAPANESE
Naval intervention

MEXICAN
Border incursions

ROYAL NAVY
sail to bases in Mexico

FLAME WARS

Canada took decisive action against Russian president Vladimir Putin's 2014 military advances into Ukraine. The official Twitter account of the Canadian Joint Delegation at NATO posted a map of the Black Sea states labeled "Russia" and "Not Russia," in an attempt to assist Russian soldiers "who keep getting lost & 'accidentally' entering #Ukraine." Russia's NATO delegation responded with their own map of the region, with the tag, "Helping our Canadian colleagues to catch up with contemporary geography of #Europe." #Europe is going to be the sponsored hashtag for World War III.

Twitter was a micropublishing website that was briefly popular among journalists and politicians in the beginning of the twenty-first century before it succumbed to a horde of angry white males.

OKAY, BUT SERIOUSLY, WHAT IF

In 1988, *Spy* magazine called up the Pentagon to find out whether there were any actual plans to invade Canada.

SPY *Sir, are there any American contingency plans in the event— however unlikely—of any hostilities from the north?*

PENTAGON OFFICIAL There is no Canadian threat. [*Pause.*] There is, um, *probably* no threat.

SPY *Sir, let's say there was a* [sotto voce] *genuine Canadian threat— are there any plans to, you know, hit them before they hit us?*

PENTAGON OFFICIAL (WITHOUT CONVICTION) We have no plans whatsoever to annex any part of Canada. They are one of our best friends.

SPY *But there must be something somewhere?*

PENTAGON OFFICIAL Well, maybe down in the bowels of the Pentagon . . . But this is not something I can really talk about.

These two Canadian politicians are so in agreement that they are probably going in for a high five.

FROM THE CENTER RIGHT TO THE RADICAL CENTER RIGHT

Half the Liberals, half the Conservatives, and half the NDP.

Canada's vibrant multi-party system offers voters a variety of choice. Will citizens elect the Conservatives, who promise balanced budgets and steady social progress? Maybe they will choose the Liberals with their promise of steady social progress and balanced budgets? Or will they shift further left and choose the New Democrats who believe in balanced social progress and steady budgets? At any given point in time, Canada has one and a half electable parties.

Until recently, every Canadian politician was required to have jowls.

CANADA'S POLITICAL PARTIES

The major political parties represent a vast and diverse range of sameness. Accordingly, they highlight their differences using their favorite colors.

Except for the Liberals, whose favorite color is gray.

THE LIBERAL-CONSERVATIVE PARTY

In 1854 Sir John A. Macdonald created a political party so bland as to never alienate anyone. It was named the Liberal-Conservative Party, which sums up one and a half centuries of Canadian party politics.

UNWHOLESOME CARICATURES

In most democracies, political parties emerge to represent the interests of certain groups, like Catholics, farmers, or people who own people. But not in Canada. In 1906, visiting French academic André Siegfried described Canada's Liberals and Conservatives as "unwholesome caricatures" of real political parties, which, since they offered no meaningful alternatives to one another, were useless as democratic instruments.

If this phrase sounds familiar, it's because you might have screamed it at your TV during every single federal election.

TOO BORING TO FAIL

The Liberal Party won over two-thirds of the elections held during the twentieth century, so it is often called the "natural governing party of Canada" by several white men in red ties. This is often attributed to its "big tent" approach to politics, which is a fancy way of saying "never pissing off Québec" and "only occasionally pissing off the prairies." The party's achievements include:

- legislating marriage equality, as soon as it was politically convenient.

- promising to legalize marijuana as soon as it becomes politically convenient.

- creating Saskatchewan, a decision still questioned by many.

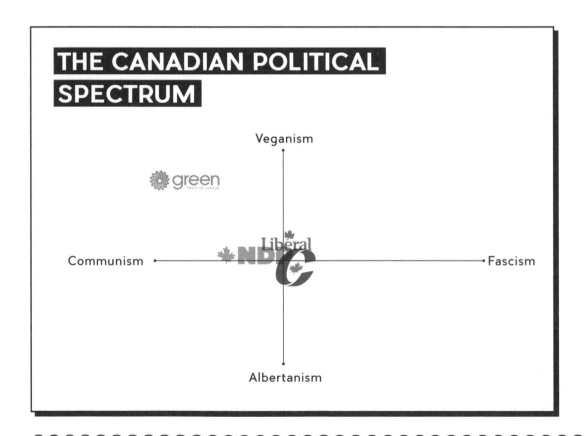

THE CANADIAN POLITICAL SPECTRUM

Veganism

green
PARTY OF CANADA

Communism ←————————— Liberal NDP C ——————————→ Fascism

Albertanism

WHERE EACH PARTY STANDS ON IMPORTANT ISSUES

Issue	Conservative	NDP	Liberal
Budget	Balanced.	Balanced soon.	Balanced . . . after a deficit.
Jobs	Make more.	Make more.	Make more . . . for young people.
Indigenous Issues	Oh, um, kinda caught us by surprise there. How about more money for education?	Jeez, didn't expect that question. I guess, we could . . . send education money to them?	Hahaha, wow. Seem to have misplaced my notes on this. Off the top of the dome, how about . . . money . . . for . . . to educate?
Legalized Marijuana	No.	Maybe.	Eventually, but not definitely.
Pipelines	Support Northern Gateway, Energy East, and Keystone XL.	Support Energy East if environmental oversight is good; oppose the pipelines people have heard about.	Support Energy East and Keystone XL, but not Northern Gateway, Lord no, never that.

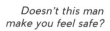

Doesn't this man make you feel safe?

OUR FANCY ROYAL HORSE BOYS

Hate crimes. Bombings. Arson. All committed by Canada's iconic "Mounties," the Royal Canadian Mounted Police. How did this union-stomping, queer-hunting, barn-burning posse of farm boys come to symbolize all that is pure and true about Canada? How do they stumble from scandal to scandal without tarnishing their benign image? With old-timey hats and animal sidekicks.

POP**QUIZ**

You've been pulled over by an RCMP officer. What do you do?

A. Offer him a sugar cube.

B. Stroke his long, luxurious mane.

C. Make an off-color remark about an ethnic minority.

D. Rub his back while making gentle shushing sounds.

When approached by an RCMP officer, stand perfectly still and do nothing, lest you get kicked in the face.

Answer: A

From 1995–2000, Disney controlled the licensing rights to the Mounties, and Mickey infiltrated Goofy's gay immigrant communist terror cell.

OUR PARANOID, INCOMPETENT SECRET POLICE

Canada's great pride and respect for the Mounties is evidenced by how we force them to stand still as decorations at public events.

Canada realized something was wrong with the RCMP in July 1974 when RCMP Constable Robert Samson blew his fingers off while handling a faulty bomb. Samson admitted to planting the bomb, and at trial, he claimed he had been told to do "much worse" for the RCMP.

Reports of RCMP wiretapping, illegal break-ins, secretly opened mail, bombings, and arson soon flooded the media. Numerous inquiries revealed that the RCMP had morphed into a secret police organization that gave itself sweeping powers to fight any (usually leftist) group that it deemed a threat to Canada.

Instead of reading accused criminals their rights, RCMP officers recite a favorite passage from Alice Munro's Lives of Girls and Women.

The Mounties were stripped of their surveillance and counterintelligence powers in 1984 and a new intelligence outfit, CSIS, was created to fuck with people. Since then, the Mounties have carried on largely as a tourist attraction that blows off steam by harassing drug addicts.

BEFORE THEY WERE FEDERALLY GELDED, THE RCMP ALSO:

Imagine how much worse it must be to be brutalized by someone who looks like this.

FORCED PEOPLE TO WATCH GAY PORN

In the 1950s and '60s the RCMP tried to root out all homosexuals in the civil service by strapping thousands of them into the "fruit machine," a device that pointed subjects' faces at photos of naked men and measured the dilation of their pupils.

BASICALLY INVENTED GRINDR

The only place in Ottawa not marked with any red dots: the RCMP station.

In 1963, the same RCMP unit produced a map of Ottawa on which the homes of suspected homosexuals were marked with red dots. The map was soon so full of red dots that it became useless. They made a few larger maps before giving up.

INFILTRATED TUPPERWARE PARTIES

In the 1950s and '60s, the RCMP regularly sent spies to Tupperware parties to root out freshness-obsessed anarchists.

SOLVED PROBLEMS WITH ELEGANT SUBTLETY

In 1972, the RCMP had a hunch that Québec nationalists were planning to meet members of the Black Panther party in a Montréal barn. When they were unable to infiltrate the barn to install surveillance bugs, the RCMP set fire to it instead to force the radicals to meet elsewhere. The barn didn't burn down, so they torched it again. The RCMP later admitted to committing four hundred illegal break-ins between 1970 and 1978.

The Black Panthers and Québec separatists ended up not meeting in the barn.

AND THEY WEREN'T FINISHED

THEY FAILED TO STOP CANADA'S LARGEST MASS MURDER

In 1985, a bomb exploded on a flight from Montréal to Delhi, killing all 268 Canadians on board. The RCMP had tracked the Sikh militant group as they planned the crime, and CSIS agents had even heard a test detonation of the bomb design that would eventually destroy the aircraft.

When asked about the incident, an RCMP spokesperson slipped on a banana peel before being crushed by an ACME anvil.

THEY USED PENSION PLAN DOLLARS TO PAY FOR GOLF VACATIONS

In 2004, the RCMP admitted that it had been using millions of dollars of the force's pension plan to pay for "laptops, computers, language classes . . . golf green fees, fudged hotel bills, gifts," and "travel."

The vacations were made all the more expensive by the officers' refusal to dismount from their horses.

THEY MISIDENTIFIED A LAW-ABIDING CANADIAN AS A TERRORIST

In 2006, the RCMP admitted they had mislabeled Canadian Maher Arar an Islamic extremist, causing US officials to deport him to Syria, where he was tortured for more than ten months. They later leaked false info to the press suggesting Arar really was a terrorist in order to cover their tracks.

Ottawa is the seat of political power in Canada, and it is ripe for the picking. Whether you're a French insurrectionist, a homegrown Islamic extremist, or simply a busload of teenagers protesting abortion, here is how to sack and occupy Canada's capital and, thus, the entire nation.

INVADING PARLIAMENT

A. THE BUBBLE Although it's not widely known, the Parliament Buildings have an invisible force field of perceived urgency. This force field—or bubble—transforms petty nonsense into real issues of substance that must be dealt with immediately. To accomplish anything of value here, you must penetrate this bubble without getting trapped in the vacuous bullshit of "the Hill."

B. PEACE TOWER This phallic symbol of Canada's national inferiority complex measures 302 feet and 6 inches. A zoning bylaw prohibits surrounding buildings from exceeding 150 feet. Once you hoist your revolutionary flag atop the Peace Tower, you will always have the biggest erection.

C. CENTENNIAL FLAME Use it to reenact the fire that destroyed the first Parliament Buildings in 1916.

D. PARLIAMENTARY LIBRARY During a firefight, your squadron can cower behind the library's elegant steel doors.

E. KEVIN VICKERS Whether you are a lone-wolf extremist with a rifle or a peaceful middle-aged protester in a foreign country, beware this man.

F. THE SENATE Do not underestimate Canada's Senators, who have nothing else to do but to remain vigilant, and are in peak fighting form after spending thousands of dollars on personal trainers.

G. HOUSE OF COMMONS   The House has already been targeted by several national security threats, including a teenage page with a protest sign and Members of Parliament. Waltz right in or just wait for members to go on a break, which happens every two weeks and all summer.

CLIMATE CHALLENGES

Ottawa's winters are as oppressive as you are, future overlord. It has some of the country's coldest, snowiest winters, with an average snowfall of 236 centimeters. It also ranks in the top ten for hottest, most humid summers in Canada. It is the worst of both worlds. Do yourself a favor and conquer Ottawa in the spring or fall, then vacation in Florida like everybody else.

RIDEAU CANAL

This waterway is a UNESCO World Heritage site, even if the United Nations refuses to officially recognize you as rightful ruler. In the winter, 7.8 kilometers of the canal are used for ice skating by the locals. The canal is a perfect place to deposit dissenters.

CANADA DAY IN OTTAWA

Like any despot, you will need to adapt to local customs to maintain stability. Keep your iron grip by hiring the Barenaked Ladies or Avril Lavigne to play a free public concert on the Hill.

REWRITE HISTORY

Glorify yourself in Ottawa's fourteen national museums. Roughly 7.3 million people visit the capital region each year and millions more will come to worship at your altar. Force the Royal Canadian Mint to only press coins with your visage. The Canada Aviation and Space Museum should show the latest in ballistic missile technology on loan from your friends in North Korea. The National Gallery of Canada should showcase only boring art that makes people feel comfortable, so no changes needed there.

QUOTE**SQUARE**

"The City of Ottawa possesses some good hotels, at which good accomodation can be found at a reasonable price, and is in telegraphic communication with every part of the United States and Canada."

—*Hunter's Ottawa Scenery*, 1855

If you walk into a room and see this man, leave.

POLITICAL SCANDALS

anadians ignore the scandals of our elected officials because demanding accountability would first require learning about Canadian politics. Be a scandal fiscal, sexual, or narcotic, the best strategy for surviving it is to hope an American politician does something even worse to divert attention. No scandal has brought down a federal government since 1873, which must make each successive prime minister wonder just how much it's possible to get away with.

QUOTE**SQUARE**

"Canada is a Northern European welfare state in the worst sense of the term . . . Canada appears content to become a second-tier socialistic country, boasting ever more loudly about its economy and social services to mask its second-rate status, led by a second world strongman appropriately suited for the task."

—Future prime minister Stephen Harper, June 1997

"Second world strongman" is also what they call unlicensed Stephen Harper Halloween costumes.

A SHORT HISTORY OF CANADIAN SCANDALS

TUNAGATE (1985)   Under the sway of StarKist, a Fisheries minister approved the sale of a million cans of rancid tuna (which is different from other cans of tuna somehow). StarKist was eventually forced to pull out of Canada. Sorry, Charlie.

AIRBUS AFFAIR (1993–95)   A former prime minister, fresh out of office, accepted three cash-stuffed envelopes from Karlheinz Schreiber, a German arms dealer. Somehow it took fifteen years for the government to conclude this was "inappropriate."

Also, he fucked an airbus.

SPONSORSHIP SCANDAL (1996–2004)   Millions of dollars earmarked to "promote federalism" were funneled from the Liberal government to ad agencies, and then back to the Liberal Party. Some of the money was used to pay for promotional golf balls autographed by the prime minister, which surely destroyed the separatist cause for good.

Civil war. Golf balls. Whatever keeps your country together, right?

ROBOCALLS (2011)   During a federal election, voters in 247 ridings received automated calls directing them to polling stations that didn't exist. Some calls were traced to a number registered to "Pierre Poutine." The only person ever charged for any aspect of the scandal was a twenty-three-year-old Conservative staffer.

Rejected names for Duffygate: L'Affaire Duffy; DuffScam; Dufftanic; The Apprenticeship of Duffy Check-Taker; Forget It, Jake, It's Dufftown.

DUFFYGATE (2012–2016)   Conservative party comfort object Mike Duffy was suspended from his dream job as a Senator for life by racking up dubious expenses. The prime minister's fanciest henchman, Nigel Wright, cut Duffy a personal check for $90,000 to repay the expenses. Duffy was charged with taking a bribe; Wright was never charged with offering one. Duffy was found not guilty.

CRONY CAPITALISM

The vast majority of corruption in Canada is just a bunch of chill bros doing each other a solid or two.

The Family Compact was called that because it comprised dozens of wealthy men compacted into a large brick-shaped mass of writhing bodies (see also: Luncheon Loaf).

This dates back to the 1800s with the Family Compact, a brotherhood of antidemocracy bureaucrats/businessmen/legislators who helped each other out by helping themselves to everything. They called themselves "gentleman capitalists." Their opponents called them "a petty corrupt insolent Tory clique." Both were right.

The spirit of the Family Compact lives on in today's corporate culture of dudes helping dudes. It doesn't matter if you're a partner at a Bay Street law firm, a Member of Parliament awarding no-bid contracts, or a board member at a government-backed bank, you'll find a helping hand if you're an entitled white dude with the right friends.

GENERAL ROT

In 2011, Canada was ranked the worst of the G7 nations at fighting bribery. Kickbacks and bribes are so common in Canada they are rarely considered scandalous. Rather, they are a part of our heritage:

THE PACIFIC SCANDAL $350,000 in political "donations" was sent to the Conservative party in exchange for a lucrative railway contract in 1872. This country was built on illicit money transfers.

TAX HAVENS An estimated $170 billion is currently languishing just out of the reach of the CRA.

EHEALTH 166 people were awarded salaries over $100,000 to digitally convert all medical files for the Ontario government, and it still didn't happen.

ORNGE Who needs all the vowels when you can have shady helicopter ambulance contracts?

SNC-LAVALIN Allegedly $47.7 million in bribes! Warsaw Pact levels of bribery!

CANADA'S BULLETPROOF SCANDAL SUPERSTARS!

PRIME MINISTER PIERRE TRUDEAU Told his opponents to "fuck off" in Parliament, but convinced everyone he had actually said "fuddle duddle."

CALGARY MAYOR RALPH KLEIN Drunkenly stormed into a homeless shelter and yelled at everyone for being lazy while throwing change on the floor. Admitted to drinking a bottle of wine a day. Re-elected.

TORONTO MAYOR ROB FORD Smoked crack on video, trampled an elderly woman in City Hall, and spoke in Jamaican patois. Were he still alive, he'd likely win a landslide victory.

It was a shocking about-face on his campaign pledge to smoke elderly women and trample crack.

TREAD LIGHTLY ON ME

If you memorize the entire Charter of Rights and Freedoms, the Governor General gives you a sticker.

CANADIAN CHARTER OF RIGHTS AND LIMITATIONS

That's right, Zoroastrians, we're on to you.

In Canada, you can practice any religion that is not deemed a threat to national security. You can peacefully protest if you are in the right place at the right time. If charged with a crime, you have access to a fair trial, provided you haven't annoyed the Americans. This is all written down on a piece of paper that stipulates individual rights and where they don't apply.

RIGHTS AND FREEDOMS FOR ALL! (EXCEPT IN QUÉBEC)

According to the Saskatchewan Pulse Growers Association, the Charter of Rights and freedoms has a "troubling" lack of references to peas, lentils, and fava beans.

The Charter of Rights and Freedoms was introduced in 1982 by Prime Minister Trudeau (the first). While Americans have snuggled with their rights for over two hundred years, prior to the charter, our Bill of Rights wasn't constitutional and could be amended or ignored on a whim. Québec has never approved of Trudeau's charter. In classic Québec fashion, they just use their own. Brian Mulroney, Canada's Ronald Reagan, made two attempts to ratify the charter in Québec, leading to the separatist fervor of the '90s.

OUR SAFE WORD IS "REASONABLE"

Canadian rights and freedoms are optional. Two clauses in the charter give the government the right to revoke the whole deal. The limitation clause notes that your personal rights can be infringed upon under "reasonable" circumstances. The charter ends with the "notwithstanding clause," which says rights 7 through 15 can be revoked for up to five years at a time, meaning citizens might not be able to secure counsel, might not get a fair trial, or might even be subject to "cruel or unusual punishment."

Lawyers generally advise against signing contracts with an "and all of this is bullshit if we say so" clause.

SECTION 2: THE LAST RESORT FOR RACISTS SINCE 1982

Does "free expression" extend to calling the entire province of New Brunswick a bunch of braindead honkies? Stay tuned for the answer in R. v. Canadaland *Book.*

We don't have "free speech" in Canada. What the Charter offers instead is "free expression," which is weaker and is diluted further by complicated libel laws, draconian copyright laws, and a general reluctance to say things that are too mean.

You're allowed to say anything in Canada as long as you can express it through interpretive dance.

WHAT TO DO IF YOUR CHARTER RIGHTS ARE VIOLATED

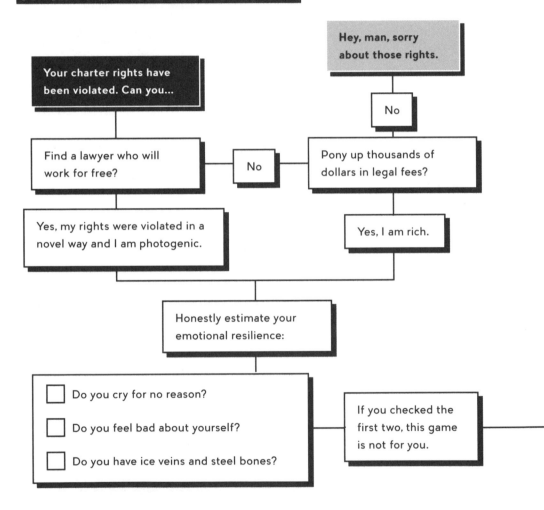

Hey, man, sorry about those rights.

Your charter rights have been violated. Can you...

No

Find a lawyer who will work for free?

No

Pony up thousands of dollars in legal fees?

Yes, my rights were violated in a novel way and I am photogenic.

Yes, I am rich.

Honestly estimate your emotional resilience:

☐ Do you cry for no reason?

☐ Do you feel bad about yourself?

☐ Do you have ice veins and steel bones?

If you checked the first two, this game is not for you.

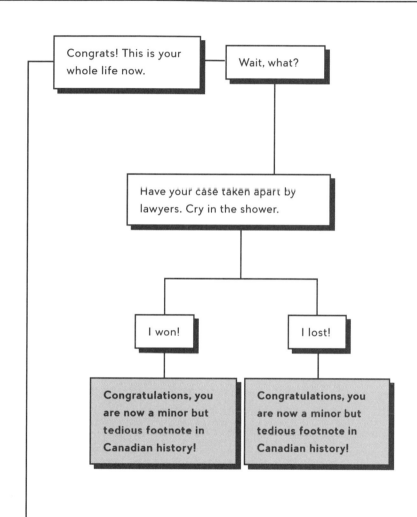

The Supreme Court of Canada does all its work from this fancy Ottawa hotel.

THE SUPREME COURT

anada's legal system was plagiarized from the United Kingdom. Common law is our language, and decisions from 1066 A.D. still carry weight. Our Constitution is full of snappy lines like:

It shall be lawful for the Queen, by and with the Advice and Consent of the Senate and House of Commons, to make Laws for the Peace, Order, and good Government of Canada.

To figure out what any of that means, the federal government tests its boundaries of authority by playing chicken with the Supreme Court.

COMMON LAW CHIC

Like our passive-aggression and lack of edible food, the Canadian judiciary's attire harkens back to our British origins. Take a moment to understand and appreciate our judges' rich history of looking like Dickensian Santas.

SUPREME FASHION

A cowl to be used whenever you visit your sick grandmother, or when you need to look adorable while sentencing someone to life in prison.

Tri-pointed hats, although rarely worn, tell a plaintiff, "You can trust me with your life."

Sashes are an excellent place to hide liquor, especially when you have to hear a case about Manitoba egg-trading wars. Yes, that's a real thing.

The Supreme Court is not air-conditioned, but luckily you can let your mare liberum get some fresh air, quid pro quo.

Every Supreme Court robe is manufactured from at least sixteen baby deer and/or ducks.

Unlike most Commonwealth top courts, the Supreme Court does not wear wigs. "Nothing in this act abrogates or derogates the full display of lustrous, radiant judicial hair," reads the 1982 Constitution Act.

COURT GESTURES

Justices are forced to retire when they reach seventy-five years of age or begin to "exhibit frequent, repeated and non-contextual flatulence from the bench."

Canadian courtrooms adhere to British-ish judicial traditions, from special titles to playing dress-up. Here are some dos and don'ts for the courtroom:

- Lawyers in many courts are required to wear black gowns that represent the impartiality of law or the inevitability of death.

- Judges don't use gavels—they yell when they need your attention.

- Depending on location, the presiding judge must be addressed as "Master" or "Your Worship" (or "My Dude," if you feel lucky).

SUPREMELY ABSENT

Save for one regrettable six-month period in the 1880s, when Canadian legal precedent was decided by horse combat.

In the early days, the Dominion of Canada didn't have a highest court to call its own. Instead, we deferred to the British Judicial Committee of the Privy Council (aka, the grown-ups). Without its own high court, the nation had the luxury of violating constitutional principles until a messenger from London made it over without getting scurvy.

INFOBOX

When Prime Minister Stephen Harper tried to appoint Québec Federal Court judge Marc Nadon to the Supreme Court, the court said no. Furious, the prime minister's office issued a press release saying he would not take the Chief Justice's phone call. Perplexed, the Chief Justice said she was not planning to call him.

SUPREME COURT JUSTICES

WHAT LIES BENEATH THEIR FLUFFY RED ROBES?

The Honourable William Rogers McIntyre

One hundred flasks of rye

The Honourable Rosalie Silberman Abella

Another set of fluffy robes

The Honourable Jean Beetz

Batman costume

The Honourable Louis-Philippe de Grandpré

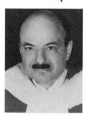

Three kids stacked on top of one another

The Right Honourable Beverley McLachlin

Full-sleeve tattoos

The Honourable Morris J. Fish

Fish

By law, the Supreme Court is required to have at least three justices from Québec. The court must also have at least one straight man, one brunette, and one lovable rogue.

The Court currently has five male justices and four women. This was most evident in the contentious 5-4 decision of Machine guns v. Ponies.

John Diefenbaker on a beach in Barbados circa 1977.

OUR PRIME MINISTERS: ARE THEY FUCKABLE?

It is said that power is the ultimate aphrodisiac. If this is true, then Canada's prime ministers are moderately sexy men and one foxy woman. While some leaders have powers like vetoing laws, ordering air strikes, and mind control, Canada's prime minister is empowered to give away mid-level positions in the civil service. Please try not to climax while reading this section.

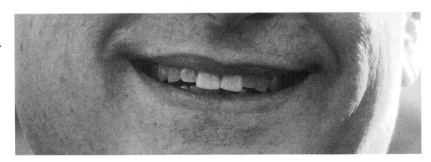

Sorry about this.

A FUCKABILITY INDEX OF CANADA'S PRIME MINISTERS

PIERRE TRUDEAU

Pro: Snappy dresser

Pro: Gonna declare martial law on that ass

Con: Thick, 1970s dad bush

Con: Going to declare martial law

Assessment: Pretty fuckable

ROBERT BORDEN

Pro: On the hundred-dollar bill

Pro: Mustache a real clit/prostate tickler

Con: Pretty racist

Assessment: Somewhat fuckable

Con: Also on the hundred-dollar bill: someone looking through a microscope for a cure for diabetes.

JEAN CHRÉTIEN

Pro: Will treat you wrong

Pro/Con: His face broke during a blizzard

Con: Hands like big freaky coconut crabs

Assessment: Hey, you got to give it to the guy, kind of fuckable

Bonus: As of press time, this one's not dead yet!

LESTER B. PEARSON

Pro: Nice boy

Pro: Universal health care, pension plan, forty-hour work week; brought you an understated bouquet of flowers

Con: Imagine screaming "Lester"

Assessment: Oh, go on then, throw the poor kid a fuck

CHARLES TUPPER

This is almost certainly the only Canadian prime minister to ever have an animal nickname.

Pro: Because of his treatment of the ladies, nicknamed "The Ram of Cumberland"

Con: Nicknamed "The Ram of Cumberland," because of his treatment of the ladies

Assessment: I don't know about this one, but I'd probably not fuck this guy if I were you

JUSTIN TRUDEAU

Con: Into hot yoga

Con: Is a scrub with fuccboi tattoos

Con: Insists on constant unbroken eye contact during sex

Con: Has already written you a sonnet after first date

Assessment: Nope

WILLIAM LYON MACKENZIE KING'S OKCUPID PROFILE, USING HIS OWN WORDS

MY SELF-SUMMARY

"I do not like my appearance . . . a little fat round man, no expression of a lofty character . . ."

MY PERSONAL PHILOSOPHY

"I've always found that you can control people better if you don't see too much of them."

54 · Ottawa, ON
100% Match

I'M REALLY GOOD AT

"Far more has been accomplished . . . by preventing bad actions than by doing good ones."

I SPEND A LOT OF TIME THINKING ABOUT

"We must nevertheless seek to keep this part of the Continent free from unrest and from too great an intermixture of foreign strains of blood, as much the same thing as lies at the basis of the Oriental problem. I fear we would have riots if we agreed to a policy that admitted numbers of Jews."

ON A TYPICAL FRIDAY NIGHT I AM

"Every hour of useful work is precious."

Another thing Mackenzie King wrote about in his diary: his belief that he could save Hitler from evil.

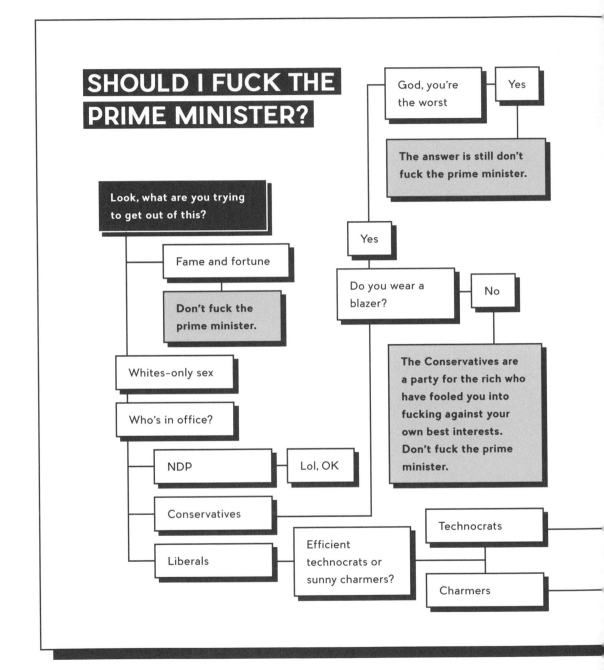

SHOULD I FUCK THE PRIME MINISTER?

God, you're the worst — **Yes**

The answer is still don't fuck the prime minister.

Look, what are you trying to get out of this?

Fame and fortune

Don't fuck the prime minister.

Yes

Do you wear a blazer? — No

Whites-only sex

Who's in office?

The Conservatives are a party for the rich who have fooled you into fucking against your own best interests. Don't fuck the prime minister.

NDP — Lol, OK

Conservatives

Technocrats

Liberals — Efficient technocrats or sunny charmers?

Charmers

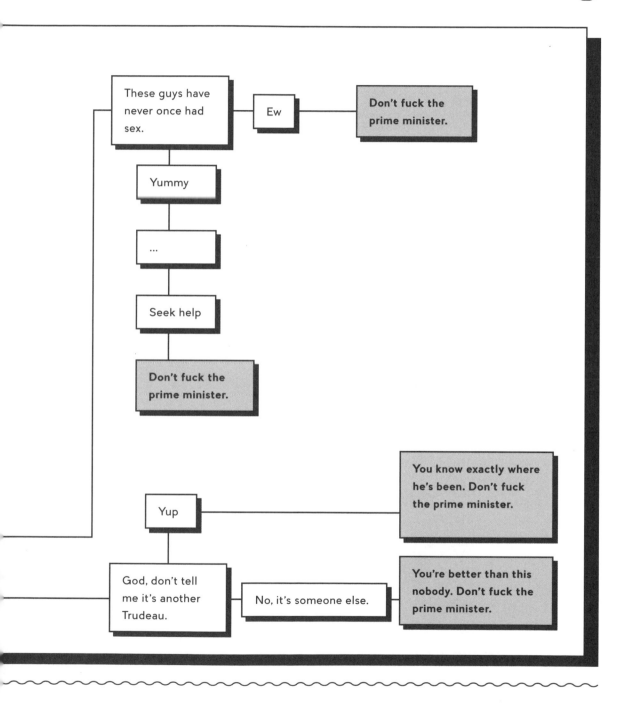

These guys have never once had sex.

Ew → Don't fuck the prime minister.

Yummy

...

Seek help

Don't fuck the prime minister.

Yup → You know exactly where he's been. Don't fuck the prime minister.

God, don't tell me it's another Trudeau.

No, it's someone else. → You're better than this nobody. Don't fuck the prime minister.

PRIME MINISTER WRESTLING MOVES

THE CHRÉTIEN CLUTCH

THE TRUDEAU ELBOW

THE HARPER FORCE CHOKE

THE MACKENZIE KING
SPIRIT BLAST

**THE PEARSON
PEACEKEEPER**

THE MACDONALD
PUKE BLAST

THE PEOPLE YOU'LL MEET HERE

500 YEARS OF OPPRESSION, THE GAME

The object of the game is to be the first Indigenous person in Canada to achieve middle-class status! Race through the obstacles of family income, educational attainment, home overcrowding, health problems, suicide, and environmental degradation to achieve moderate success!

Indigenous rates of illness are exponentially higher than those of non-Indigenous people, due to generations of exposure to poutine, colonialism, and Hudson Bay sweaters.

In 2016, the Supreme Court of Canada declared that Métis and non-status Indians were considered Indians under the Constitution Act, sharing with them the gift of oppressive wardship given to their First Nations and Inuit cousins.

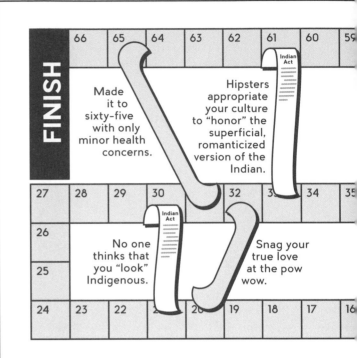

FINISH

| 66 | 65 | 64 | 63 | 62 | 61 | 60 | 59 |

Made it to sixty-five with only minor health concerns.

Hipsters appropriate your culture to "honor" the superficial, romanticized version of the Indian.

Indian Act

| 27 | 28 | 29 | 30 | | 32 | 33 | 34 | 35 |
| 26 |
| 25 |
| 24 | 23 | 22 | 21 | 20 | 19 | 18 | 17 | 16 |

Indian Act

No one thinks that you "look" Indigenous.

Snag your true love at the pow wow.

Game pieces

First Nations
Belong to tribal nations, live on reserves, universally love fry bread.

Inuit
Originally from the far north in Canada, fierce survival skills, hate PETA.

Métis
Descendants of European men and Indian women, distinctive culture, will brag about sash.

Urban Aboriginal
Live in the city, super-political, probably a vegetarian due to their hunting skills.

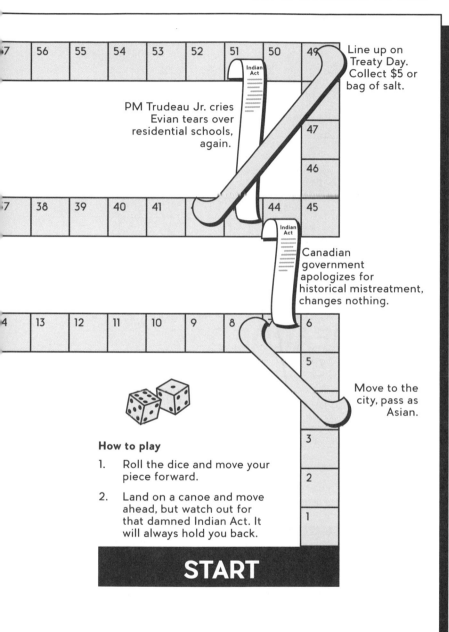

On Treaty Day, the Crown provides annual payment to registered First Nations individuals in exchange for ongoing occupation of their land. Examples of annual payment include: $4, $5, a bag of salt, a loaf of bread, cheese.

After apologizing to former students of Indian residential schools, Prime Minister Harper proceeds to erode Indigenous rights, self-determination, land claims, languages, and culture over the next seven years.

Line up on Treaty Day. Collect $5 or bag of salt.

PM Trudeau Jr. cries Evian tears over residential schools, again.

Canadian government apologizes for historical mistreatment, changes nothing.

Move to the city, pass as Asian.

How to play

1. Roll the dice and move your piece forward.

2. Land on a canoe and move ahead, but watch out for that damned Indian Act. It will always hold you back.

START

Hockey is an elegant and beautiful game, meant to foster teamwork, leadership, hand-eye coordination, and a laid-back attitude toward physical assault.

OUR SMELLY, MOIST, PATCHY-BEARDED ICE GOONS

You just saw a big, angry-looking guy launch himself at another guy and attempt to gouge his eyes out. Someone just skated past you with a mouthful of blood. Also, some guy just body-slammed another guy's head into a pane of Plexiglas, causing him to be carried off the ice on a stretcher. Everyone on the ice is fourteen years old. Their parents are watching and also fighting each other. It's hockey, Canada's favorite sport!

INFO**BOX**

In hockey, both enforcers must agree to a fight. E-vites are still considered gauche; by post is best.

A LIST OF CANADA'S MOST TERRIFYING PEOPLE

MINOR-LEAGUE HOCKEY COACHES

Youth hockey in Canada allows body contact starting at the Atom (age nine to eleven) level. If you talk to minor-league hockey coaches, this is when *real* hockey begins. To prepare their players for physical hockey, these fully grown adult men will often command nine-year-old children to get out there and "start hitting," "get in the corners," and "get rough"— all code words for "beat the shit out of the other children." Players who have second thoughts about this are often told to "man up" and stop being sissies, under threat of decreased playing time.

Other things that will get you called a sissy in hockey: complaining about a concussion, wearing a visor, being European.

HOCKEY PARENTS

As terrible as coaches may be, they have nothing on hockey parents, who routinely assault other adults in front of their own children. In 2014, a Winnipeg mom and dad were banned from coming to their son's games after getting into a fight with the opposing team's coaches. After a minor-league hockey game in Osoyoos, BC, in 2016, a large crowd of parents from both teams began fighting in the stands. Hockey parent "rink rage" has become so bad that some leagues have experimented with forbidding parents from making "any negative noise" during games.

GOONS

Hockey historians argue that the rapid expansion of the NHL between the '60s and '80s created room for less-skilled, more-physical players whose sole purpose was to intimidate opponents. Coaches get these "enforcers" to focus less on athletics and more on remaining physically intimidating, and on seeking out fights with other teams' goons. While star players go to sleep the night before a game thinking about strategy, enforcers stay up worried about entering into a violent confrontation with another six-foot-eight, two-hundred-fifty-pound monster.

HOW TO FIX FIGHTING IN HOCKEY

BAN   Goalie fights, bench-clearing brawls, lying to an opponent about how you will catch them during a trust fall.

MAKE FIGHTS SHORTER   If a player appears to be in serious danger during a fight, the referee should step in to help deal the finishing blow.

ENCOURAGE EARLY FIGHTING   Not teaching your kids how to fight by the time they start playing Midget hockey should be illegal.

MAKE FIGHTING OFF THE ICE LEGAL   Many players are surprised to find out that physical assault is illegal off the ice. Chicago's Patrick Kane was indicted on multiple misdemeanor charges and given a conditional discharge after he allegedly punched a cab driver over twenty cents. Toronto's Tie Domi fought a fan during a game. Cut down on the confusion by making it legal.

ALLOW FIGHTING WITH INANIMATE OBJECTS   Sometimes a fight will spill off the ice and into the streets, like in 2011, when angry hockey fans in Vancouver began fighting mailboxes, store windows, police cars, etc.

DON CHERRY'S TOTALLY NONRACIST HOCKEY PLAYER HIERARCHY

As legendary hockey broadcaster and "Greatest Canadian" Don Cherry attests, "There is no racism in hockey!" Here are his nonracist beliefs about people of different ethnic backgrounds in hockey.

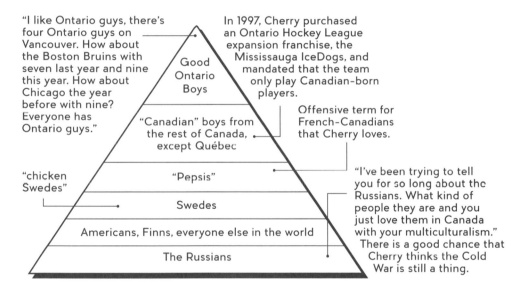

"I like Ontario guys, there's four Ontario guys on Vancouver. How about the Boston Bruins with seven last year and nine this year. How about Chicago the year before with nine? Everyone has Ontario guys."

In 1997, Cherry purchased an Ontario Hockey League expansion franchise, the Mississauga IceDogs, and mandated that the team only play Canadian-born players.

Good Ontario Boys

"Canadian" boys from the rest of Canada, except Québec

Offensive term for French-Canadians that Cherry loves.

"chicken Swedes"

"Pepsis"

Swedes

Americans, Finns, everyone else in the world

The Russians

"I've been trying to tell you for so long about the Russians. What kind of people they are and you just love them in Canada with your multiculturalism." There is a good chance that Cherry thinks the Cold War is still a thing.

Pictured: two Canadas.

Do you have a moment to talk about the invisible forces that shape our world?

OUR INTELLECTUAL CHARLATANS

You can blame Canada for the modern scourge of TED-talking, airport-book-writing idea-hustlers who market think-nuggets as "game-changing" epiphanies. Canadians invented the art of PowerPoint-packaged positivity.

Not only are many of today's speaking-circuit gurus Canadian, but the whole concept of the marketable rock-star intellectual is itself Canada-born.

Professor Marshall McLuhan of the University of Toronto was (according to the *New Yorker*) "the world's first pop philosopher." His ideas percolated into journalism, TV, and advertising. "Advertising is the greatest art form of the twentieth century," he told *Advertising Age* magazine in 1976.

McLUHAN TRANSLATOR

"The medium is the message."	The small is the text, and the large is the e-mail. The extra-large is a dollar more.
"The new electronic interdependence recreates the world in the image of a global village."	We will have a global village full of stolen credit card numbers where you can send strangers death threats.
"Psychic communal integration could create the universality of consciousness."	I'd like to buy you a drink but I don't understand human interaction.
"Native societies did not think of themselves as being in the world as occupants but considered that their rituals created the world and keep it operational."	I've never met these "natives" but I hope this sounds like I have.

Instead of writing his own books, Marshall McLuhan would lie on a sofa and let loose a stream of free association that his assistants would scribble down. Some of his babble seems to have brilliantly predicted the Internet. Other aphorisms reveal that he was just throwing shit at the wall to see what would stick. For example, "Invention is the mother of all necessities."

In honor of McLuhan, this is also how this chapter was written.

Not everyone was fleeced. American critic Dwight Macdonald described McLuhan's writing as "impure nonsense, nonsense adulterated by sense." The *New York Times* called his writing "horrendously difficult to read, clumsily written, frequently contradictory, oddly organized, and overlaid with their author's singular jargon." McLuhan was famously dismissive of his critics and maintained that they just didn't get it, man.

"You and I are archetypal degradations of a preceptual modality that puts apprehension before obsolescence." —McLuhan dumping his college girlfriend

"I'm gonna put my ideas into you."

A LEGACY OF BIG IDEAS

DOUGLAS COUPLAND   Canadian novelist, artist, and media guru who popularized terms like Gen X and McJob.

"The Tipping Point" is also the name of a thrilling pleasure known only to a select core of Gladwell Groupies.

MALCOLM GLADWELL   It can cost up to $1,300 per minute to have him speak about *The Tipping Point*, *Blink*, or any of the cool psychological quirks Gladwell has discovered that can revolutionize your dental practice or management consultancy.

NAOMI KLEIN   The child of Vietnam draft dodgers, Klein is the author of the antiglobalization manifesto *No Logo*, which is known for its very distinctive cover logo. Books like *The Shock Doctrine* and *This Changes Everything* are loathed by economists for their simplicity and beloved by environmentalists despite taking hundreds of pages to describe one-page concepts.

If Malcolm Gladwell gave paid talks for 10,000 hours at $1,300/min, he would have $780 million.

RICHARD FLORIDA   Technically, he is not a Canadian. But Toronto adopted him when he flattered the city as a prime global example of "the Creative Class™." His genius lies in telling urban, Internet-adept creatives that urban, Internet-adept creatives are the most desirable people on planet Earth.

POP QUIZ

MARSHALL McLUHAN CONCEPT OR JUST TWO RANDOM WORDS SLAMMED TOGETHER?

A. Mechanical Bride
B. Holistic Plane
C. Typographic Man
D. Lukewarm Warm
E. Truck Gardens

F. Robotic Eyeball
G. Mood-Mud
H. Digital Gestalt
I. Bonanza-land
J. Archetypal Banality

McLuhan: a,c,e,g,i. Made-up: b,d,f,h,j.

#1 National Bestseller

Safe

By the author of THINKING IS FUN

*

Quirky, Bland Ideas That Your CEO Will Love

"...wonderful speaker. Would book him again in a heartbeat."
—American Dentists' Association CEO Howard Bland

Canada's bestselling book.

Welcome to Toronto, a large North American city. The way you'll know that you're here and not in Chicago, Philadelphia, Detroit, or a dozen other places is that there's a very tall tower right downtown.

WHY SO UGLY?

"We're Canada's largest railroad company. What could we build that best represents that?"

"How about the world's tallest TV antenna?"

Toronto was labeled a "temporary city" for the first years of British rule. As it grew in the nineteenth century, this Protestant backwater turned to meatpacking as its primary industry. You actually needed a special license to buy liquor for personal use until 1969, and some neighborhoods maintained prohibition until 1994.

But in the '60s and '70s, fear suddenly made Toronto the center of Canada's universe. Companies terrified by the possibility of a sovereign Québec moved their head offices from Montréal to the next best option. They were soon followed by equally terrified Anglos (English-speaking Montréalers).

Seemingly overnight, Toronto boomed. At the exact ugliest moment in the history of architecture, construction exploded, with no regard for urban planning or aesthetics of any kind.

QUOTE**SQUARE**

"It's not a good-looking city. You've got all the worst architectural fads of the 20th century. That's crypto-fascist Bauhaus. Mussolini would have been perfectly at home in that one. Looks like every public school in America. And every third-tier public library."

—Noted media ego and chef Anthony Bourdain

WHAT DO I DO HERE?

Very good question!

HOW TO FILL THE VOID

Ever had a shawarma the size of a preemie? Toronto has! How about poutine with pork three ways? You betcha. Fourteen-day green juice cleanse? They're right next door! The city has a particular penchant for novelty baked goods, pretentious fusion, and the needlessly wheatless. Since the city's food is the only thing that has ever brought residents any semblance of joy, they stuff chow mein burritos in their mouths like they're not all on the slow, inevitable road to oblivion.

MUNI-CENTIPEDE: AMALGAMATION'S REVENGE

Toronto is a composite of boroughs and cultures stitched together ass-to-mouth. After decades of unhindered suburban sprawl, Toronto's many bedroom communities were suddenly "amalgamated" into an incoherent and ungovernable behemoth in 1998. Want to extend the subway system by a few stops? No problem! That will be done in twenty years or so.

LIKE SPORTS BUT HATE WINNING? TORONTO IS THE CITY FOR YOU!

Toronto loves its professional sports teams, but its professional sports teams hate Toronto. Ticket prices to watch the Leafs, the Raptors, the Blue Jays, or Toronto FC play are the highest in the country. Yet there have been a total of fifteen championships won over almost a hundred years. Sports in Toronto is an epic experiment in human behavior to see how much people will pay to be humiliated and disappointed before they lose interest (hasn't happened yet).

CULTS

Clans of brainwashed weirdo misfits led by charismatic narcissists tend to seek out extreme, remote places, far from normal people, where they will be generally left alone. Quality cults gravitate to Florida, the rest end up in Canada.

QUOTESQUARE

"I believe the world needs more Canada."

—Bono

OUR TOP CULTS

RAELIANS

Topless recruiters for this alien sex cult can be found at most Montréal summer festivals. Founded in the '70s by a French race car driver named Claude. He previously tried to set up in Israel, but his choice of a swastika for a logo kind of fucked that up. After putting the swastika inside a Star of David didn't work either, he built his compound in swastika-neutral rural Québec. He briefly scored some media attention for lying about having cloned a human and for establishing an elite order of religious prostitutes.

This is an example of really terrible branding.

THE CHILDREN OF GOD

While they were founded in California in 1968, the Children of God—a group of fundamentalist Jesus freaks—wasted no time heading north. They set up in Vancouver with ninety converts. Their popularity may be due to "flirty-fishing," which involves having sex with members of the general public to encourage conversion.

Who is doing the logos for these cults?

VICE MEDIA

VICE was a Québec welfare-grant scam that has since expanded into a media empire worth at least $2.5 billion. VICE founder Shane Smith has declared his brand a cult and referred to its young adherents as "sweatshop" laborers, whom he has openly disdained for relying on their parents' wealth in order to accept sub-subsistence wages. Like many cults, VICE demands absolute loyalty, rewards the faithful with coveted rings, and constantly glorifies drug use.

Okay: #1 fuck, #2 marry, #3 kill.

Lululemon founder and thigh gap measurer Chip Wilson.

LULULEMON: TOTALLY NOT A CULT!

By introducing high-performance butt-enhancing sportswear to yoga in 1998, Lululemon founder Chip Wilson helped dissociate the ancient practice from breathable natural fabrics, religious tradition, and philosophies emphasizing selflessness. He ushered in an age of competitive meditation among anxious, overachieving type-A white women. Under Wilson, the organization was notoriously cultish, mangling Eastern philosophy to school its employees in a sort of libertarian, pranayama-meets-the-übermensch philosophy where creepy inspirational mantras and "clearing" sessions are the norm. Anyone advancing to a managerial level was "strongly encouraged" to participate in the Landmark Forum. Also, they once gave anyone who would stand naked in front of their store for thirty seconds free clothes.

KEY CONCEPTS

CLEARING   If an employee shows up to work at a Lululemon store and their manager thinks they're in a bad mood, that employee is asked to go through "clearing," whereby they spill the beans on their personal life and receive "coaching" from their boss.

CHIP WILSON   Founder Chip Wilson believes that child labor is acceptable because it gives poor kids jobs, that feminism and the pill made women stressed out and that's why they want to do yoga, and that women without thigh gaps shouldn't wear his company's leggings.

THE LANDMARK FORUM   A for-profit self-help organization that uses techniques eerily similar to brainwashing to bring participants in line with its Baby Boomer empowerment philosophy. Highly litigious, so we apologize for and retract the previous statements about the Landmark Forum, a highly respected seminar series embraced by organizations around the world, whose only goal is to improve the lives of its participants.

A Lululemon event, where yoga is imagined by Leni Riefenstahl.

Would you buy drug policy from this man?

DRUGS!

Canadians are known for good manners, friendliness, and a squeaky-clean image. We also love producing, transporting, distributing, and consuming drugs. Next time you're hanging out with a Canadian, remember: those good manners were honed during sketchy drug deals. We're friendly because we're high as fuck.

QUOTE**SQUARE**

"(Inaudible) . . . I know (inaudible) . . . (inaudible) . . . (inaudible) . . ."

—Rob Ford

EXPLAINING CANADIAN
BEHAVIOR WITH DRUGS

Your Vancouver barista takes forever to make your macchiato and then accidentally drinks it.

Ha ha, sorry about that dude. Canadians smoke about 1.7 million pounds of (mostly locally grown) marijuana per year.

1.7 million pounds EACH!

You cut in line at Safeway and nobody complains.

The guy behind you could have said something, but instead he eased back into his soft clonazepam haze and immediately forgot about it. Canadians are also among the world's biggest consumers of synthetic opiates, and are dropping dead from fentanyl abuse on the daily.

You ask someone for directions, they give you an emotionally intense backrub and some Pixy Stix.

It could be old-fashioned Canadian friendliness. Or it could be the fact that we manufacture most of North America's MDMA.

You greet a Toronto bus driver. He smiles and tells you that he has just witnessed the universe's creation.

In Canada, it's illegal to possess psilocybin mushrooms when they're dried. So long as they're consumed fresh—picked from a verdant pasture, say—you have nothing to worry about.

OUR GREATEST EXPORTS

This ship is leaving Vancouver packed to the brim with drugs.

Very dynamic. Almost too dynamic. Canada is a dynamic player in a free-trading global economy. Our trading partners include:

AUSTRALIA AND NEW ZEALAND   Our Commonwealth brethren love our sweet Canuck ecstasy. About 80 percent of the love drug imported into Australia and New Zealand comes from us.

COLOMBIA   Canadians are great at shoveling snow. With southern borders becoming more difficult to cross, Colombian crime syndicates are now shipping cocaine by air and sea to Canada, where we dilute it before sending it elsewhere.

All of the cocaine imported into Canada is responsibly grown and ethically sourced.

THE USA   British Columbia alone brings in $8 billion annually shipping high-grade cannabis to the United States, which is more money than is earned by the province's softwood lumber trade.

THE USA, AGAIN   Remember our business with the Colombians? Most of that cocaine ends up in American nostrils.

STILL MORE USA   If you're grinding your teeth in an American club, there's a very, very good chance those amphetamines came from Canada.

HERITAGE MOMENT

TORONTO MAYOR ROB FORD

Toronto Mayor Rob Ford was a cartoon character invented by Canada's top ad agencies as part of a national antidrug program. The zaftig mayor of Toronto was featured in a series of public service anouncements in which he abused drugs and alcohol with disastrous and zany results. In one characteristic PSA, Mayor Rob is at an eatery drunkenly speaking in Jamaican patois. This PSA was followed by a voice update from lovable Mayor Rob saying that he was drunk on "his personal time" and not on drugs. In a later PSA, Mayor Rob checked into rehab, which taught Toronto kids a powerful lesson of redemption as it applies to rich, white men.

A family of Canadian white people attends a Leonard Cohen concert.

MULTICULTURALISM

Canada is renowned for its diversity and multiculturalism. Travel a short distance outside of any city and you will find a vast and varied spectrum of white people. Canada's white peoples have developed distinct cultures and regional practices. Most are named Gordon.

INFOBOX

White people from Prince Edward Island have thirteen different words for "potato." One of these words requires the speaker to literally hold out a potato, an item which all Islanders carry as an amulet against harm.

REGIONAL DRESS

Kokanee hat

Oakleys

Heavy-duty jeans

Timberlands

KELOWNA, BRITISH COLUMBIA

Alexander Keith's hat

HALIFAX, NOVA SCOTIA

Soft hands

Molson Hat

Fireball breath

Upper-body injury

Labatt hat

North Face fleece

Tim Hortons ulcer

AJAX, ONTARIO

WINNIPEG, MANITOBA

CULTURAL PRACTICES

DRIVING LARGE VEHICLES

Even white people who do not haul lumber, tow heavy loads, or participate in manual labor of any kind own large trucks and SUVs.

Popular Canadian white people tradition: stabbing trees until they bleed, boiling their blood, and then consuming it for breakfast.

JUNIOR-LEAGUE HOCKEY

Like many ethnic majorities, Canada's white peoples worry their kids will assimilate and forget their roots. Junior-league hockey steeps young white children in their heritage and is a bulwark against the encroaching mainstream.

GIVIN' 'ER AND GOING OUT FOR A RIP

In certain enclaves, white people practice the tradition of givin' 'er, while other communities are known to go out for a rip. In either case, this means getting drunk with your buddies. Whether it's a mickey (a flask) of screech (moonshine rum) in the Chi (pronounced "she," short for Miramichi) or a two-four (a case) of pops (beers) in Etobicoke, there is rarely a "her" present, and going out for a rip in your mother's basement counts as "out."

Canada's vulnerable white cultures are endangered by growing external pressures. These include: petitions to get rid of fighting in hockey, feminist critiques of video games, the Extreme Pita fast food chain.

RELIGION

There are many denominations of white people. Places of worship include Irish pubs, Home Depot, and "Canadian-Chinese" restaurants. The white man bible is *The Game* by Ken Dryden (Old Testament) and *The Game* by Neil Strauss (New Testament).

CANADIAN DIVERSITY TIMELINE

1807 The Royal Montreal Curling Club opens, allowing white people to scream at rocks sliding on ice, an activity they still enjoy to this day.

1867 Thirty-six white men get so drunk that they invent Canada.

1885–1923 Canada passes eight different Immigration Acts aimed at protecting Canadian diversity from Chinese, Japanese, and Eastern European people.

1971 Prime minister and benevolent white person Pierre Trudeau solves Canadian racism by announcing multiculturalism as an official government policy.

2015 An Australian elections strategist convinces Canadian white people that the niqab is a problem in Canada.

HOW TO BEHAVE

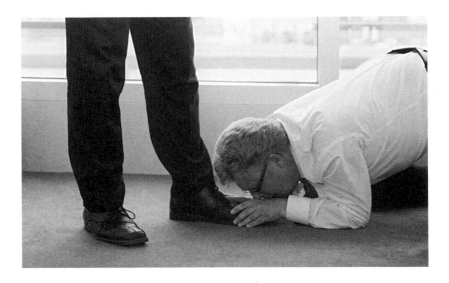

ETIQUETTE

Canadians are famously polite, humble, and modest, according to themselves. This reflexive and often disingenuous tendency toward self-effacement has found expression in a codified set of cultural norms referred to as Canadian "manners."

And if you don't agree, then fuck you!

BEHAVIOR**QUIZ**

A mother stumbles over a curb and inadvertently throws her infant into the air. It's coming your way. Do you:

A. Catch it and return it to the mother.

B. Raise your hands and stand absolutely still so witnesses can attest that you did not touch the child.

Answer: A

Notice how whenever Canadians say "sorry," they never specify WHO should be sorry.

"APOLOGIZING"

Canadians rarely apologize. Yet utterances of the word "sorry" are so ubiquitous that they seem like an involuntary tic.

The word "sorry" comes from the Old English word "sarig," meaning "pained" or "distressed." When Canadians say they are "feeling sorry," they are telling you that they feel uncomfortable.

Sorry.

The meaninglessness of a Canadian apology has actually been enshrined in law. The 2009 Apology Act states that the phrase "I'm sorry" does not constitute admission of fault or liability and cannot be entered into evidence in a civil proceeding.

SORRY, TRANSLATED

SCENARIO 1

"Sorry," says a man to a panhandler who has just asked him for a dollar to get some food.

Translation: If you talk to me again I will call the police.

In colonial times it was customary to apologize whenever you murdered an entire subspecies of buffalo.

SCENARIO 2

"I'm sorry, but when you described the brunch special, didn't you say these would be *wild* blueberries?"

Translation: You are a liar, and I am dedicating my afternoon to ruining you on Yelp.

SCENARIO 3

"Sorry, I don't speak French."

To compensate, French Canadian people never say sorry.

Translation: And why should I? You have put me out of my depth and humiliated me. Why don't you secede already?

SCENARIO 4

"Sorry!" says a man to the fire hydrant he just walked into.

Translation: I defer to you, solid object.

SCENARIO 5

"The Government of Canada now recognizes that it was wrong to forcibly remove children from their homes . . . and for this we are sorry," says Prime Minister Stephen Harper to Canada's First Nations.

Translation: As my speechwriter will later confirm, this apology is a strategic attempt to kill the story of how the Canadian government practiced cultural genocide against Aboriginals. Let there be no mistake: In six years' time, I will extend the brutal policies of my predecessors by underfunding Aboriginal education.

EYE CONTACT

Many Canadians have eyes. See if you can match the city to its eye-contact style:

1. Toronto

2. Montréal

3. Vancouver

4. Calgary

A. Fleeting eye contact is acceptable when you encounter another runner before six a.m. Never, ever sexual in nature.

B. Nods of hetero solidarity or an exchange of manly squints are appropriate when your SUV or pickup is stopped at a red light next to one of identical make and model.

C. It is considered rude for strangers not to eye-fuck each other when passing on the sidewalk.

D. Eye contact between strangers in public settings may constitute assault.

1-D, 2-C, 3-B, 4-A

WHAT CANADIANS WEAR

Canadians often wear clothes. Our citizens take pride in covering up their bodies. As they should. However, despite their best efforts, only 2 percent of our citizens are actually well dressed. The rest of the country can be found wearing the same set of clothes from the same set of stores.

1. LULULEMON HIGH-TIMES FULL-ON LUXTREME YOGA PANT

Yoga-inspired athletic apparel from the mind of Ayn Rand-loving Chip Wilson. Lululemon helps fit, toned, conventionally attractive Canadian women remain fit, toned, and conventionally attractive.

2. WHITE MESH BODYSUIT/ SHIRT THING: AMERICAN APPAREL BANKRUPTCY SALE

Everyday Walmart basics at three times the price, originally brought to you by Dov Charney, a Montréal boy with the personality of a porn recruiter. Pre-ruin, American Apparel tried to sell your 12-year-old daughter crotchless tights by telling her she was supporting ethical labor practices.

3. CANADA GOOSE PARKA

The perfect coat to wear to the store to buy chips in totally seasonable temperatures. If the coyote-fur lining helps arctic hikers survive, then it should be good for your run to the dep.

4. JOE FRESH SOCKS

Sharp, simple clothes at a fair price. The company kept costs low via cheap labor and shoddy safety standards. Bangladeshi workers making Joe Fresh clothing were killed in a 2013 factory collapse. Joe Fresh passed that loss of life on to the fashion-savvy Canadian to convert Western guilt into stylish savings.

5. ROOTS OLYMPIC POORBOY CAP

The Roots poorboy cap is a baggier, felt-ier take on the Kangol or other driver-style caps of the time. Consider yourself Samuel L. Jackson's embarassing northern cousin.

6. SOREL BOOTS

If you want your feet to smell like festering garbage, strap into a pair of these clunky bad boys. Bonus: These shoes are so improbably cumbersome that you get to waddle around cleared sidewalks like some kind of crippled duck.

This Canadian is about to go out for a night of drinking.

THE TRUE NORTH IS DRUNK AND NEEDS TO PEE

Both the Saint Lawrence Seaway and the Rideau Canal were designed, financed, and constructed during extended whiskey blackouts.

Canada drinks 50 percent more than the rest of the world, and yet we have some of the most restrictive and confounding alcohol policies west of the Muslim world. Each province has its own drastically different liquor laws—most of which date back to our brief World War I-era dalliance with prohibition.

Prohibition didn't last, and we quickly became America's favorite plug, shipping rivers of bootleg whiskey to Atlantic City and helping to establish the Mafia. But despite its libertine history, Canada has somehow accumulated a maze of anachronistic liquor regulations that even we can't keep straight. What's the legal drinking age? Easy—nineteen. Except where it isn't. Where can you buy booze? In Ontario, only in Soviet-style government liquor stores. In Québec, any corner store will sell you a beer, but not liquor. If you live north of Edmonton, bathtub moonshine is your new BFF. Despite every obstacle, we always manage to get shitfaced.

HOW TO BUY BOOZE IN CANADA

You'd think it would be easy to purchase booze in a country as full of degenerate drunks as Canada. You would be wrong. Until 1975, customers at Ontario's government-run liquor stores had to sign their name every time they bought booze, and each store was provided with a list of drunks who were not allowed to shop there. (As a prank, many Ontarians took to writing down the name of the head of the United Church of Canada.) In 1985, Canada finally struck down the Lord's Day Act of 1906, which prohibited the selling of liquor (and anything else) on Sundays. In most provinces, it is still impossible to buy alcohol after five p.m. on weekends.

Canadian things that don't make sense sober: curling, National Film Board movies, the Calgary Stampede, New Brunswick.

CLEAR EYES, FULL BOTTLES, THIS SUCKS

In Canada, you are not actually allowed to show someone drinking a beer in a beer commercial, nor can you imply that the product will at all alter a person's consciousness or "improve a person's quality of life" in any way.

No word yet on depicting vodka enemas.

As per Canadian Radio-television and Telecommunications Commission rules, any bottles that appear in advertisements for alcoholic beverages must be full, so as not to imply the act of drinking. Active verbs like "buy" or "drink" or "have" cannot be applied to the product, and must be replaced with passive formulations like "Why not buy . . ." Advertisements "must not imply that the product will help you escape from life's problems."

These restrictions help explain Labatt's most well-known slogan, "If you could buy Labatt at some point that would be awesome."

Pigeons enjoy the cool, refreshing taste of Molson Canadian beer.

RIGOROUS STANDARDS AND CASUAL SEXISM, COURTESY OF MOLSON CANADIAN

To skirt liquor advertising regulations, Molson, makers of our nation's most popular beer, has targeted the vast douchebag demographic.

If inebriated Canadians absolutely must relieve themselves on a war memorial, Veterans Affairs Canada advises selecting a monument for the Boer War or lesser.

"What to drink when you're chasing beaver."

—2005

"You clap for the dancer, even though she shouldn't be a dancer."

—2008

"You've turned down a booty call in the post-season."

—2009

CANADA: A NATION BORN OF DRINK

The practice of transcribing parliamentary debates was begun largely so Macdonald could remember who he'd told to fuck off.

The Maritimes joined Canada because everyone got so drunk at the 1864 Charlottetown Conference that they couldn't not join after a rager like that. The meeting had a $200,000 champagne budget. John A. Macdonald was so hungover he couldn't even stand up for an official portrait.

DRINKING ABROAD

The only thing Canadians love more than drinking at home is traveling abroad and getting shittered there.

PUERTO VALLARTA

Every year, almost two million Canadian citizens visit Mexico. Online reviews of Mexican resorts are replete with complaints about "drunken Canadians," "disrespectful Canadians," and "utterly wasted Canadians." One recent review of a Puerto Vallarta resort complains that "the 'adult relaxation' pool did not allow children but it allows loud and obnoxious drunken Canadians." (*National Post*)

"Lissenammee. You fuck—you think . . . fuck you," remains the leading retort by Canadians cut off at Mexican resorts.

LONDON

In 2005, the Canada Day street party in London, UK (billed as "one of the largest gatherings of Canadians outside Canada"), was described by city police as a "nightmare" of drunken disorder. According to the *National Post*, "By the time the party was over, three people were in hospital, and three were in police custody. There was no beer for many blocks around and Maiden Lane itself was a 'mattress of broken glass.'" A police sergeant remarked: "Two guys turned up with a picnic table and an icebox at 11 o'clock in the morning and they were still there at 11 o'clock at night."

Canadian drinking humor: (To a vomiting Canadian) "Excuse me, were you drinking Caesars or is your digestive system hemorrhaging?"

INFOBOX

- 62 percent of Canadians regularly binge drink.
- 63 percent see no problem with their drinking habits.
- 64 percent think the definition of "binge drink" is what needs changing.

More than 200 bilingual New Brunswickers are killed every year by reading Stop/Arrêt signs as a double negative.

BILINGUALISM(E)

Canada has two official languages: English and French. Everything from government documents to airplane announcements to the label on a jar of mustard (*moutarde*) must appear in both languages. Except in Alberta, where French translations simply appear as English with the word "le" in front.

COMFORTING LES CANADIENS

From the start, nobody was happy. After annexing New France in 1760, the British tried not to piss off their new Francophone subjects, and so they let them practice Catholic traditions—guilt and fake abstinence—without interference.

Ottawa bureaucrats are known to experience recurring nightmares in which they forget to answer the phone with "hello bonjour."

As with any compromise with the British, the other party realized they had been shafted after a deal had already been reached. French was recognized as equal in status to English in the House of Commons, Senate, and the courtroom, but not as an official language.

"Is it not wonderful?" wrote George Brown, one of the Fathers of Confederation, in 1864. "French Canadianism entirely extinguished!"

OFFICIAL LANGUAGES ACT

One hundred years later, the government looked into relations between "the two founding races" of Canada and discovered that Francophones indeed still existed and were still getting shafted. Under Prime Minister Pierre Elliott Trudeau, bilingualism became official.

English businesses complained that printing all those extra labels would rid their companies of English customers and French antagonism. French people complained that they would have to learn English to even benefit from the policy. In the end, nobody was happy.

Prior to this, Canada employed a form of the British Languages Act, which was just a parchment scroll reading "SPEAK ENGLISH."

ALL THE GOOD SWEARS ARE FRENCH

Québec's best swears are all about the Catholic church. Yell any of these in a row to pay homage to the holiest of holies—saying fuck in a new language.

TABARNAK

English meaning: tabernacle. Pronounced: tah-bear-knack.

OSTI, HOSTIE, OR ESTIE

English meaning: host, the bread used during communion. Pronounced: oh's-tee.

CÂLISSE

English meaning: chalice. Pronounced: ka-lease.

CIBOIRE

English meaning: the container that holds the host. Pronounced: see-bwarrr.

Imagine that your church featured a priest delivering sermons from atop a "cuntbag" and offering blessings with a "fuckbadger." That's sort of what all this is like for Francophones.

SACRAMENT

English meaning: sacrament. Pronounced: sac-ra-mon

More than Canada, less than Europe. A city of cobblestones and potholes, wine in convenience stores, and unsettling levels of street clowning. If you like good food, civil unrest, high art, common-law marriage, beautiful architecture, and endemic corruption: *bienvenue*!

INFO**BOX**

Buildings in Montréal are not allowed to be taller than the top of nearby Mount Royal, which features a giant steel cross that overlooks the city. But again, totally secular place!

WHERE TO GO

THE OLD PORT The city's historic port dates back to the early 1600s, when French fur traders employed it as a trading post. Today you can catch an IMAX flick there and weep at the city's neglect of the district's crumbling, ancient buildings.

THE MAIN The beating heart of Montréal, Boulevard Saint-Laurent—the city's main strip—was the historical dividing line separating the city's working-class French in the east from the working-class Anglos in the west.

PARK EX Follow the city's tearful trail of migration north to the borough of Villeray–Saint-Michel–Parc Extension, aka Park Ex. Ride the 80 bus for four hours until you arrive smack in the center of Québécois cool. Live like a local artist, weed dealer, or grad student by dining on cheap Pakistani food and drinking overproof beer in Jarry Park.

Visit this thing before it completely disintegrates!

FILL THE VOID WITH

SMOKED MEAT   Kosher-style *viande fumée* is perhaps the singular, go-to Montréal delicacy. The surly authenticity of Schwartz's Deli is almost worth the wait until you realize the joint is owned by Céline Dion.

STEAMIES   A *steamé* is an artisanal sausage made from various cuts of pork, beef, and/or chicken, lovingly boiled and grilled, placed in a delicious, fluffy bun, and garnished with vinegar-based tomato puree and mustard seed sauce. At eighty cents each, they're available on any street corner.

POUTINE   This Québécois fast-food dish—thick potato fries topped with gravy and squeaky cheese curds—is Montréal's gift to the world. Poutine is best enjoyed in the time-honored Montréal style: purchased blind drunk at four a.m. and jammed, half-eaten, in the refrigerator overnight, then begrudgingly gobbled down the subsequent afternoon while excruciatingly hungover. Pairs well with lukewarm Diet Pepsi.

All the best food in Canada looks like shit.

WHAT TO DO

TAM-TAMS Montréalers gather every week in Mount Royal Park to fill the air with the beats and baps and boom-boom-bips of amateur drumming. They also fill the air with the scent of stepped-on hash, beeswax candles, and body odor.

NOTHING The very fact that you are consulting a travel guide tells me that you're a loathsome Anglo who likes to ruin everything by planning for it. Put down this guidebook and live your fucking life for once. Go get laid by a French person.

GET CHIDED BY A FRENCH CANADIAN FOR SPEAKING BROKEN QUÉBÉCOIS FRENCH The look of contempt you'll get from a Francophone—say, when you ask for *l'addition* at a restaurant when you want your bill, as one might in France—is one of the city's most beautiful views.

ENJOY HIGH CULTURE From cinema to comedy to music to whatever FrancoFolies is on about, arts festivals are inescapable during the few months of the year when Montréal is not frozen. If you enjoy lining up for things or squeezing your body through densely packed mobs to watch jam bands noodle on free public stages, this is the place for you.

LEAVE Montréal is the most charming and sexy city in North America. It is sophisticated, civilized, and cheap. After a weekend visit or a university degree, many will try to stay. Remember: you may love Montréal, but it will never love you back. *Au revoir*!

CANADIAN SEXUALITY

In which case, why bother?

If you find the British not quite repressed enough, come to Canada. Oral sex was illegal until 1969 and anal sex is still illegal in most provinces if more than two people are present. Erotic comic books are regularly seized at the border, stripping is illegal in Saskatchewan except for charity, Nova Scotian teens are prohibited from taking nude pictures of each other, and there is not one person in Manitoba you want to see naked. To make up for all of this, there's Québec.

INFOBOX

"A Canadian is someone who knows how to make love in a canoe," quipped Pierre Berton, the beloved Canadian writer. Before arriving at that gem, Berton discarded these early drafts:

" . . . someone who gargles balls on a snowmobile."

" . . . someone who is anally pleasured whilst represented by a Westminster-style parliamentary democracy."

CANADIAN SEX SCANDALS

BABY'S FIRST SEX SCANDAL

In 1966, Gerda Munsinger, a blond German prostitute and alleged KGB spy, was revealed to have seduced several members of Prime Minister Diefenbaker's cabinet, including the associate minister for national defence. The press hoped the Munsinger affair would change Canada's "dull and unexciting" image and bring more tourists to Expo 67.

Expo 86 would have employed the same strategy, but an elderly Gerda Munsinger declined to participate.

DIEF THE (DEADBEAT DAD) CHIEF

In 2011, forty-two-year-old George Dryden went public with the claim that he was the love child of former prime minister John Diefenbaker. The claim was highly suspect, as Dryden's only proof was significant DNA overlap with John Diefenbaker, a mom who used to fuck John Diefenbaker, and the fact that he looked exactly like John fucking Diefenbaker.

THESE ARE RESIGNING WORDS

Albertas solicitor general Graham Harle took his title very seriously. After a police officer found him outside a seedy Edmonton motel with a prostitute, he claimed to be on the job, investigating the problem of prostitution. His investigation, he said, had concluded that prostitution "didn't appear to be a problem right at the moment." Asked why he hadn't told the police or his office about this, he said, "I didn't know that, obviously, until I made some inquiries, did I?"

AND THAT'S IT

Every other Canadian sex scandal would probably be better described as simply a "scandal."

CANADASUTRA

HOW TO FUCK LIKE A CANADIAN

The following lewd acts have been recognized by the federal government of Canada.

THE GROUP OF SEVEN

THE UPPER CANADIAN

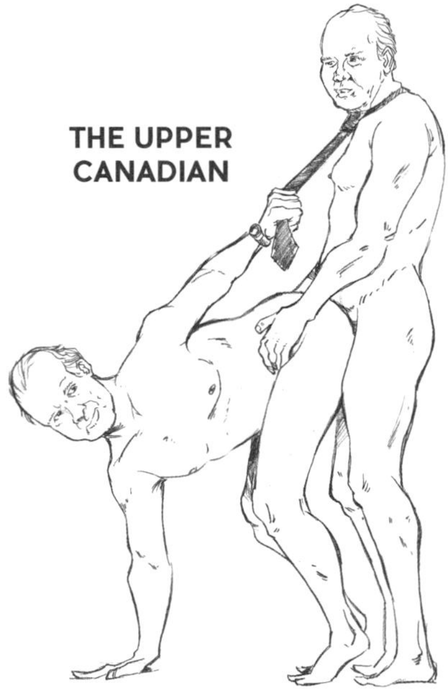

THE FURRY TRADE

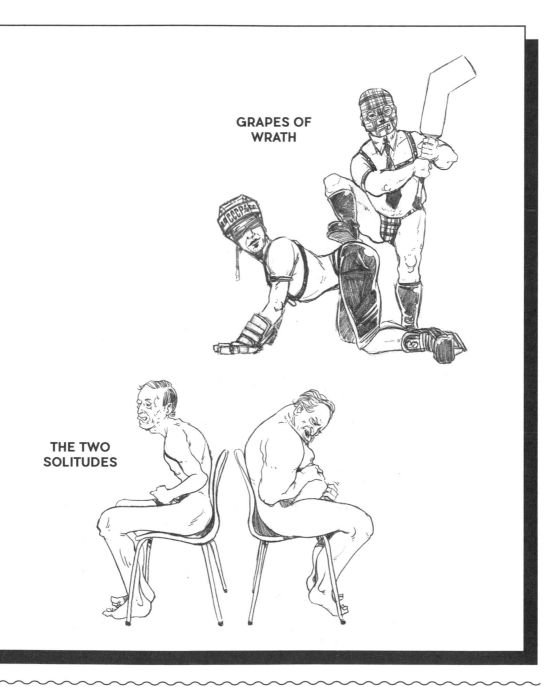

GRAPES OF WRATH

THE TWO SOLITUDES

FAMILIES

Family values and lots of child labor in the 1800s.

Canada is a nation built on family values. At times we have ripped children away from their mothers, but only when we thought it was in their best interest to speak Canadian or if the Catholic Church could make a buck from the deal.

Anyhow, we said sorry for all that.

These days we give people tax breaks for reproducing. Yet Canadians are refusing to get knocked up enough to maintain the population. Women are waiting longer and longer to have kids, and then they're having fewer kids than ever. Are Canadians an endangered species? And if so, who cares?

Yes, that's right, tax breaks. This book pays for itself.

HERITAGE MOMENT

CANADA'S STORK DERBY

n 1926, a deranged Canadian millionaire left $9 million in his will to the Toronto mother who had the most babies in a ten-year span. To stop the ensuing Stork Derby, the government tried to have the money donated to the University of Toronto but was accused of communism and being boner killers. At the end of a decade, it was left to a judge to decide which of thirty-two families had won. This Depression-era version of *The Biggest Loser* resulted in a tie across six families who each received between $200,000 and $2 million.

Inspired by the success of paying people to have kids, the Canadian government got in the family way. In 1934, the Ontario government drummed up some major revenue by kidnapping the Dionne quintuplets. They made the five baby girls into wards of the Crown because their parents were found to be "unfit." The government built a special hospital for the girls where they could be raised in the loving environment of complete strangers, and tourists came from all over North America to gawk at them. At age nine, the quintuplets were reunited with their parents in a rural, Catholic Northern Ontario town. They stopped speaking to their parents the second they turned eighteen.

EVERYTHING YOU NEED TO KNOW ABOUT CANADIAN FAMILIES

 In 2005, Canada became the fourth country to legalize gay marriage. The other three were the Netherlands (tall), Belgium (cultured), and Spain (can also get it).

 It's illegal to sell your sperm in Canada. Because Canadian men will only masturbate for money, there is a donor shortage. Canadian uteri are mostly being fertilized by imported American sperm.

This was all part of an American ploy to annex Canada.

 Of the 3.7 million couple-families with children, 87.4 percent are considered "intact," with all kids counted as offspring of both parents.

 One in ten children lives in a stepfamily arrangement because Daddy made a mistake and Mommy is all out of forgiveness.

 The most typical family arrangement in Canada is a childless couple, with over 40 percent of couples reporting no kids at home, sex on demand, and spare cash for vacations.

 While the median family income is $78,000, the best family to be in is one that includes a married middle-aged white man who earns upward of $191,000. If you're that guy, congratulations! Sorry your kids don't appreciate you.

 More than three-quarters of families with one child over the age of six own at least one pet. His name is Lincoln, he's house-trained, loves playing outside but gets tired easily, and is actually a human grandparent.

TIME OFF TO AVOID YOUR FAMILY AND OTHER STATUTORY HOLIDAYS

The fertility rate in Canada has been in steady decline for forty years. The last year that Canadian couples produced enough children to replace themselves was 1971. The replacement rate in 2011 was 1.61. For comparison, it was 2.64 during the Depression when sex was scarce and dust filled the valleys. More women are delaying the age at which they give birth, while men are prolonging the age at which they're grossed out by childbirth. To solve this problem, the federal and provincial governments have set up a number of public holidays when the work must stop in the hope that fruitful copulation will occur.

FAMILY DAY

British Columbia, Alberta, Ontario, Manitoba, and Saskatchewan. Known as Islanders Day in PEI.

On Family Day each Canadian family may tar and feather one childless single person.

NATIONAL PATRIOTS' DAY

Québec. They always have to one-up everyone with those names.

NATIONAL HOLIDAY

Québec. They really need everyone to get to *le boning*.

CANADA DAY

Nationwide. A day for getting blindingly drunk and stumbling sideways into the bed of your future co-parent.

There is nothing less romantic that I can think of than Canada Day.

DISCOVERY DAY

Newfoundland and Labrador. Time to discover more babies.

Pictured: Toronto Raptors global ambassador Aubrey "Drake" Graham.

OTHER SPORTS

There's more to pro sports in Canada than just hockey, and if you have the heart of a champion, exceptional physical prowess, and the ability to work a few side jobs during the off-season, you, too, can be a professional athlete in Canada.

QUOTE**SQUARE**

"[Canadian cable] ain't got enough channels, but I deal with it."

— Sonny Weems (former Toronto Raptors forward)

"The cream in Oreo cookies is different."

— Othella Harrington (former Vancouver Grizzlies forward)

CURLING

HOCKEY'S DRUNKEN PARENT

Curling was created in the 1500s in Scotland and was introduced to Canada in the 1800s as a way to alleviate the crushing boredom of being a settler in pre-Confederation Canada. Hockey may be Canada's sport, but curling is the sport of Canadian dads. In curling, it's not only okay to be drunk while playing, it's encouraged.

Canada invited Scotland to tour the country in a curling tournament in 1858. Scotland accepted the invitation forty-four years later.

HOW TO CURL

1. Find three friends who are looking for an activity less strenuous than softball, but with more drinking and a higher risk of sliding face-first into a sheet of ice.

2. Find some people standing around a sheet of ice—and who have already started drinking—to play against.

3. Pick the most obnoxious person in your group to be the "skip" (ask them to scream "HURRY HAAARD" at seemingly random intervals).

4. If you're the skip, grab a rock, line up on the centerline of the ice ("sheet"), and then push the rock toward the target at the end of the sheet ("house"). The sweepers will try to control the speed of the rock ("hog head") by using their brooms ("Swiffer™") to clean the ice ("slippy slidey-widey").

One of the most popular sports in Canada involves a group of drunk people screaming and throwing rocks at a house.

5. Get your rock as close to the middle of the house as possible. If other rocks are in the way, hit them. If other players are in the way, hit them, too. When both teams do their rock-sliding thing, that's called an end—or booty.

6. The team with the most points after ten ends wins, and the other team has to buy the next round and clean the barf off the ice.

CANADIAN FOOTBALL

WE HAVE A FOOTBALL LEAGUE?

Canada's version of American football has a slightly longer field, a few rule changes, and none of the excitement, fans, or star power. Formed in 1958, the league has nine teams with names of ancient badasses (Saskatchewan Roughriders, Toronto Argonauts), of badass animals (Hamilton Tiger-Cats, BC Lions), and badass . . . whatever these are (Winnipeg Blue Bombers, Ottawa Redblacks).

We assume this is horribly racist but haven't checked.

Other possible CFL team names: the Football Players, the Roughriders.

For almost forty years, in a league with only nine teams, two CFL teams were called the Roughriders. It took one of them to dissolve for them to pick a new team name, and even then there was still talk of bringing back the Roughrider name.

FUN FACTS ABOUT THE CFL! HEY, DON'T WALK AWAY FROM ME, GET BACK HERE!

 Players regularly take side jobs to supplement their meager salaries. Calgary Stampeders fullback Scott Deibert signed with the team so that he could continue his sales job at an oil patch equipment company. Two members of the now-defunct Ottawa Renegades worked as repo men.

 In 1984, the general manger of the Winnipeg Blue Bombers forgot the Grey Cup trophy in a hockey rink after the post-final game celebration. It's like it meant nothing to him. Or to anyone.

 In 1939, the ground at the stadium where the Grey Cup was to be held was frozen and too hard to play on, so the grounds crew poured four hundred gallons of gasoline on it and set it on fire.

LACROSSE

Lacrosse started out incredibly badass but is now associated with rich white boys in boarding schools. Centuries ago, lacrosse (called *baggataway*, or "theballwentthatawaygetitbeforeitrollsintotraffic") was played by Indigenous people in southern Québec and Ontario. It consisted of anywhere from a hundred to a thousand men running around a field up to three kilometers long.

Lacrosse games lasted as long as three days or until the last player collapsed from exhaustion. Modern lacrosse games are over in time for nonconsensual homoerotic prep school locker room rituals. In the 1800s, a Montréal dentist created the first lacrosse club. Currently, the two main types of lacrosse played in Canada are field lacrosse (played on a field) and box lacrosse (played on a box).

THE LITTLE LEAGUES

RINGETTE: NOT A FEMALE ONION RING

Ringette was created in 1963 to give women something (more) to do. The sport does not allow intentional body contact and fighting is banned, which shows how little the creators knew about teenage girls.

CRICKET: THE JABBERWOCKY OF SPORTS

John A. MacDonald deemed cricket the official sport of Canada in 1867. Canada and the US had competed in the first international cricket game in 1844, which is the last time Canada achieved anything in international cricket.

MAJOR-LEAGUE SOCCER: PROFESSIONAL BEER LEAGUERS

Footballer Didier Drogba, arguably the best human playing soccer in Canada today, likely experiences everything that happens to him in Canada in slow motion.

Canada has three MLS teams—Toronto FC, the Vancouver Whitecaps, and the Montreal Impact—and superior European and South American players can jog circles around our mediocre talent. The Canadian national team is best known for coming last in everything, from CONCACAF to FIFA to those parent–child games that Under-13 teams play at the end of the season. In the two FIFA tournaments they have made it to, Canada was successful in not scoring a single goal, meaning that the national team now can best its record simply by scoring a point.

WE'RE NUMBER ONE! BECAUSE WE'RE THE ONLY ONE!

MAJOR-LEAGUE BASKETBALL

Canadian Dr. James Naismith had an idea to cut out the bottom of a peach basket and throw a ball into it. When it came time for Toronto to have an NBA team, they chose "Raptors" from the following list of names: Beavers, Bobcats, Dragons, Grizzlies, Hogs, Raptors, Scorpions, T-Rexes, Tarantulas, and Terriers. Canada has had to get by with the Raptors, who have won zero championships and are a testament to Canada's can-maybe-do-in-the-future spirit.

The first-ever NBA game was played on November 1, 1946, at Toronto's Maple Leaf Gardens, where the New York Knickerbockers beat the Toronto Huskies 68 to 66. Anyone taller than Toronto captain George Nostrand got into the arena for free so that they could play for the Huskies.

MAJOR-LEAGUE BASEBALL

Canada contributed two teams to the MLB—the Montréal Expos and the Toronto Blue Jays. The Expos relocated to Washington in 2005, leaving one team named after a shrill and annoying bird. The Jays won back-to-back World Series championships in 1992 and 1993, followed immediately by over two decades of miserable failure. They are now beloved by a legion of fans who proudly wear "I [HEART] BJs" T-shirts. The Blue Jays are worth $900 million, making them worth slightly more than the GDP of Tonga.

CANADIAN TERRORISM

Canada is unable to produce any truly good homegrown talent in the field of terrorism. Our most successful terrorists are mediocre at best. The industry faces a problem of brain drain, with all the real talent emigrating to the Middle East.

Canadian terrorism is less "terrifying" than it is "spooky."

QUOTE**SQUARE**

"Almost the entirety of Canada's territory is, and will remain, an unproductive and useless frozen wasteland . . . I wish the earthquake had engulfed that miserable Acadia instead of Lisbon."

—Voltaire (1756)

THE FENIANS

In the 1860s, Canadians feared the Irish nationalist Fenian Brotherhood. The master plan of the Fenians was to improve the conditions of the Irish by annexing Canada, a country with the highest global standard of living for Irish immigrants. After that, they were going to trade it to Britain in exchange for Ireland. The greatest success of the Canadian domestic branch of the Fenians was to assassinate MP Thomas D'Arcy McGee, whose main task in office had been to lobby for Irish Catholic rights and who was about to retire.

"Well, if it isn't the country that got INVADED BY IRELAND," is how Canadian diplomats were greeted in London until 1900.

THE AIR INDIA BOMBING

The most devastating terrorist attack in Canadian history killed all the passengers on Air India flight 182. And yet, Talwinder Parmar and Inderjit Reyat of the terrorist group Babbar Khalsa were only slightly less bumbling than CSIS and the RCMP, the law enforcement agencies who failed to stop them despite one million chances. Parmar and Reyat first allegedly tried to pay a random criminal to put the bomb on the plane, but that guy went straight to the police. They were not arrested. They were still not arrested after two others, including an RCMP informant, corroborated the story.

CSIS knew Parmar was the head of a terrorist organization. They knew he had threatened to kidnap and kill the family of the Indian Consul General. Yet they did not pull him over and search the trunk of his car after they followed him to the woods and heard an explosion. Although the airline received a tip-off, airport staff allowed the bag with the bomb to be checked in without a passenger, and explosives sweepers let the bag go through, even after their gear detected explosives. Even with all this extraordinary luck, Reyat and Parmar still managed to fuck up their plan, and one of the two bombs detonated before it could even reach a plane.

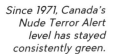

Since 1971, Canada's Nude Terror Alert level has stayed consistently green.

THE SONS OF FREEDOM

A nudist, antimaterialist splinter group of the Doukhobor sect of Russian Christians, the Sons of Freedom carried out a nude bombing campaign in western Canada from the 1920s through the 1950s. A nude bombing is like a regular bombing, only the person detonating the bomb is nude. The only deaths conclusively linked to Sons of Freedom bombs came in 1958 and 1962, when would-be bombers were killed by their own bombs. They likely got distracted by a cool breeze in the wrong hole.

THE SQUAMISH FIVE

The Squamish Five were a group of anarchist "urban guerrillas" from Vancouver in the 1980s. Their major caper was the bombing of a Toronto factory that manufactured cruise missile parts. The plan was to cripple the factory without hurting anybody, but they were bad at making bombs and their bomb went off early. Ten people were injured, while the factory itself was more or less unscathed. Before their arrest, the Squamish Five also firebombed several pornography stores in an attempt to end pornography for all time.

Alarmed by the rise in motivated anticapitalists, in the 1980s CSIS immediately began a secret government program to invent the cannabis vaporizer.

THE FLQ

A radical Québec separatist group, the Front de libération du Québec burst onto the scene in March of 1963, distributing pamphlets drawn in crayon throughout Montréal. The FLQ carried out their first bombing less than a month later and managed to slightly damage a twenty-five-inch section of railway, prompting Prime Minister Diefenbaker to say, "I'm totally unconcerned."

When asked how far he would go to combat the FLQ, Pierre Trudeau responded with the now-famous phrase "Just do it."

The largest bomb ever detonated by the FLQ was outside the Royal College of Electrical and Mechanical Engineers. It absolutely devastated one car. In one of the FLQ's most successful operations, they stole office supplies from a local NDP office.

Although the FLQ were socialists, one of their most infamous deeds was the murder of Pierre Laporte, who had been a crusader against the fascistic Duplessis regime. The FLQ did succeed in briefly turning Québec into a police state, and must therefore be given their due as terrorist pioneers.

*"1. Kill beloved politician. 2. More crayon drawings. 3. Independent Québec."
—FLQ manifesto*

Wheeeeee!!

THE TORONTO 18

Although news of a jihadist conspiracy to attack targets in Ontario shook the country in 2006, the Toronto 18 may not have done anything worse than play paintball on a camping trip while a series of police agents infiltrated their group, bought them fake bomb powder, and promised to show them how to shoot guns.

In a now-familiar pattern, this would-be Islamic terrorist attack on Canada was foiled by . . . Canadian Islamic informants. Suck on that, Geert Wilders.

Fooled by an undercover cop, the group's ringleader told his friends that a man who boasted about his martial arts skills and firearm license was "buffed up" and would "buff us up, too." During one of their training weekends in Orillia, Ontario, the group made a recruitment video that showed them daring one another to jump over a campfire, doing donuts in the parking lot of a Canadian Tire, and giggling.

OOPS! YOU'RE NOT A TERRORIST AFTER ALL

MAHER ARAR

The RCMP falsely suspected Arar was linked to terrorism and passed the bad info on to the CIA, who shipped him off to Syria, where he was imprisoned and tortured for years. When the truth started to come out, the RCMP leaked false info to the press suggesting the terrorism ties were true. Sorry!

Ha-ha, we're still cool, right, guys?

BYRON SONNE

After police stopped Sonne for jaywalking they visited his website, where he called cops "bacon." He was then charged with planning to bomb the G20 political summit. He spent eleven months in jail awaiting trial and his wife left him. He was acquitted on all counts. Sorry!

OMAR KHADR

At sixteen, Khadr was Gitmo's youngest inmate. The "confession" of a terrified child and resulting decade-long incarceration were internationally condemned. Upon Khadr's release, Canada threw him in a maximum-security prison and the federal government blocked his release. When the Liberals came into power, they reversed Canada's position on Khadr, who's now free. Sorry!

How could anyone possibly hate Canada after going through something like this?

HOW WE THINK

Until the launch of CTV in 1960, CBC's only competition for TV viewers was watching one's children die of polio.

THE CANADIAN BROADCASTING CORPORATION

The CBC is an easy-listening radio station for the elderly. It has a mixed talk-and-music format that combines upbeat chat with light jazz and salsa. The CBC also operates a website and a TV channel. Popular programs have included *Wheel of Fortune*, *Coronation Street*, hockey games, and *Simpsons* reruns.

In addition to its broadcasting activities, the CBC is a furnace of hostility where the worst human impulses and emotions are executed by way of a bloodless and stultifying bureaucracy. In this way, the CBC fulfills its mandate to reflect Canada to Canadians.

WORKPLACE

Each department of the CBC is a fiefdom ruled by a highly paid executive, locked in perpetual zero-sum conflict with neighboring chieftains for a greater share of the organization's annual federal allotment.

Radio and television hosts are the symbolic representatives of each fiefdom. The influence of each fiefdom can be determined by the number and size of posters, cut-outs, and billboards displaying the gleaming head of that fiefdom's host, as displayed in the atrium of the CBC's Toronto headquarters.

Peter Gzowski is turning in his grave, but it is no longer clear why.

Mail is delivered by robots. Bathrooms are for crying.

THE CBC'S MISSION

When describing its five-year strategic plan, the CBC stressed that it "can't be all things to all people." The name of the CBC's current five-year strategic plan is "Everyone, Every Way." The CBC describes itself as a "digital first" broadcaster, even though its digital department receives less than 5 percent of the corporation's annual operating budget.

The CBC's mandate calls for it to "reflect the multicultural and multiracial mandate of Canada." This photo reflects the type of pundit that CBC News asked to comment on the Black Lives Matter movement:

"Our ideal radio voice is whispered and slightly outraged, as if one is stoically addressing the dying grandfather who molested you."
—CBC standards manual

WHO'S YOUR DADDY?

The CBC has provided Canada with a range of father figures to fill a variety of gaping emotional holes. Take your pick:

PETER MANSBRIDGE

Nickname: Gray Poppa

Pro: Comforting and calming

Con: Frequent new mommies

A pre-James Bond Sean Connery starred in a 1961 CBC production of Macbeth. It was the last time Connery's accent made contextual sense on film.

STUART McLEAN

Nickname: Folksy Daddy

Pro: Didn't really talk that way in real life

Con: Might be dead, have to check

MICHAEL ENRIGHT

Nickname: Jazz Daddy-O

Pro: Adorably clueless about anything that happened in pop culture after the Cold War

Con: Jazz

DAVID SUZUKI

Nickname: Hippie Dad

Pro: Pleasing patchouli scent, can probably get killer weed

Con: Loses his shit when you take long showers

Every episode of The Nature of Things had to edit out at least one instance of David Suzuki saying, "Fucking donkey dick fuckfaces."

DON CHERRY

Nickname: Bigot Pop

Pro: Always on the verge of a stroke

Con: Always on the verge of a stroke

THAT DOESN'T SOUND RIGHT

WHICH OF THE FOLLOWING CLAIMS ABOUT THE CBC IS TRUE?

A. The only person allowed to express an editorial opinion on the CBC's flagship news broadcast is a climate change denier who receives checks from petroleum industry lobby groups.

B. The CBC's hippest celebrity ever was a fifty-year-old man who was acquitted of five sexual assault charges from three women, had a sixth charge from another woman dropped in exchange for a public apology to her and a "peace bond" restraining order, and was never charged in relation to the 15 other women who have accused him of assault or harassment.

C. After allegations of workplace and sexual abuse tarnished the CBC program Q, it was rebranded as q.

D. All of the above.

Answer: All of the above.

The CBC has North America's highest ratio of youth-targeted TV hosts who schedule annual prostate checks.

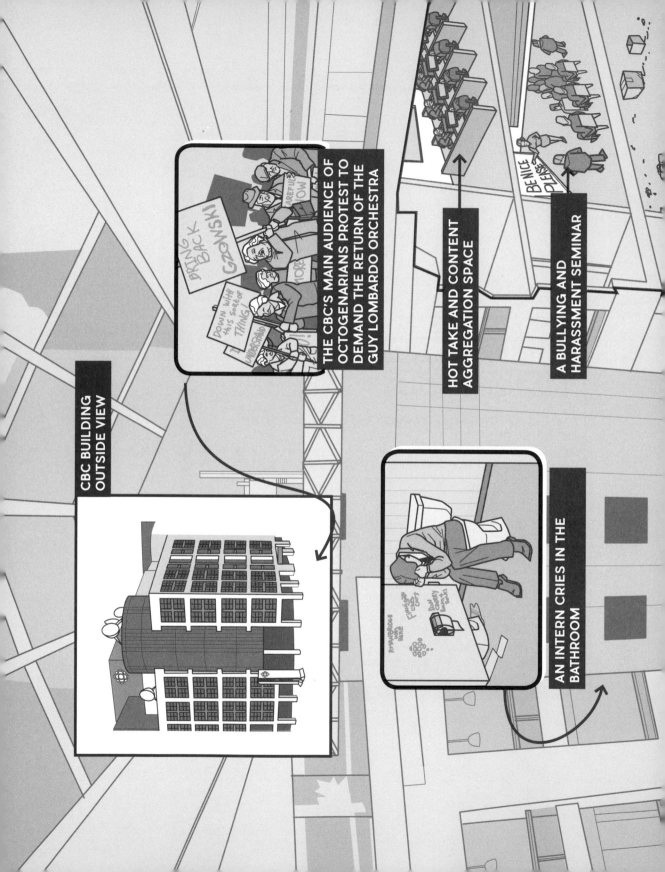

CBC BUILDING OUTSIDE VIEW

THE CBC'S MAIN AUDIENCE OF OCTOGENARIANS PROTEST TO DEMAND THE RETURN OF THE GUY LOMBARDO ORCHESTRA

HOT TAKE AND CONTENT AGGREGATION SPACE

A BULLYING AND HARASSMENT SEMINAR

AN INTERN CRIES IN THE BATHROOM

THE CBC INNER SANCTUM

The CBC headquarters is in downtown Toronto. This large gray maze with a hole in the middle — the atrium — is home to the network's biggest stars, overpaid executives, and interns.

A DISGRACED STAR ESCORTED OUT, AS HE PASSES HIS OWN POSTER

THE PRESIDENT OF THE CBC ENJOYS THE COMPANY OF HIS COLLEAGUES FROM A DISTANCE

This man was Canadian TV's biggest heartthrob for eighteen years.

TELEVISION

American companies are not allowed to own Canadian TV stations, because if they could, all they would do is broadcast American television to Canadians. As a result, all broadcast licenses are awarded exclusively to domestic broadcasters, who use them to broadcast American television to Canadians.

In exchange for this multibillion-dollar monopoly, these broadcasters agree to make a handful of state-funded Canadian TV shows as a small concession to the public good. The broadcasters don't like it and neither do Canadians, so they agree not to try too hard and we agree not to watch.

SIMPLE PEOPLE DOING MUNDANE THINGS

From *Corner Gas* to *Little Mosque on the Prairie* to *Trailer Park Boys* to *Road to Avonlea*, Canada loves (or at least tolerates) shows about simple people doing mundane things in small towns. The towns in these shows are usually made-up (Dog River, Avonlea, Wessex), little slices of rural life, set in either the Prairies (*Little Mosque on the Prairie*), Ontario (*Letterkenny, Murdoch Mysteries, The Red Green Show*), or the Maritimes (*Road to Avonlea, Republic of Doyle, Trailer Park Boys*). The people are polite(-ish), they like hockey and beer, and never think to leave Canada.

One exception was Due South, a show about a Mountie fighting crime in Chicago who never took off his dress uniform.

These people are not real. They are from a very sarcastic fictional comedy sketch.

SCTV's "Great White North" sketch is a great example of how Canadian television executives often miss the point. When *SCTV* moved to the CBC, executives complained that the best Canadian TV show of all time wasn't Canadian enough. Rick Moranis and Dave Thomas responded by loading every tired Canadian stereotype into one ludicrous sketch. "It was all very stupid," said Thomas. "We thought 'Well, they get what they deserve.'" But the irony was missed and audiences took Bob and Doug McKenzie's hoser schtick as a direct send-up of Canadians. The sketch became *SCTV*'s most popular ever, and people still do bad impressions of the duo whenever they need to mock Canadians, despite the fact that no Canadian really talks like that. Thanks, CBC management!

CANADA'S CREEPY KIDS' TV SHOWS

CAILLOU   The only TV show ever to unite an entire country in willing a small, bald child out of existence.

It took forty-three writers to come up with the name "Ananas."

TÉLÉFRANÇAIS   A French TV show about kids who hang out with a sentient pineapple (named Ananas, French for "pineapple") that lives in a scrap yard.

MR. DRESSUP   Mr. Rogers's understudy created his own Mr. Rogers-like show, including the creepiest thing on TV, the Tickle Trunk, which could only be opened by tickling it—and I feel uncomfortable just writing that.

THE RACCOONS   Ecoterrorist rodents try to stop an evil capitalist pink naked guy with a dick for a nose from polluting the environment.

Hi, I'm Caillou. Mind if I hang out in your nightmares?

COMEDY

JUST FOR LAUGHS GAGS The most successful global export of Québécois humor has been raking it in for decades by repeating one joke. That joke is "boo!"

THIS HOUR HAS 22 MINUTES Like *The Daily Show*, but for people who don't like to laugh.

ROYAL CANADIAN AIR FARCE Imagine if your parents and their friends got together to do impressions of politicians using a collection of seven wigs.

By any metric —running time, viewership, number of international spinoffs—Just for Laughs Gags is the most successful Canadian comedy TV show of all time.

This plastic novelty has a sitcom in development with CTV.

DRAMAS

ROAD TO AVONLEA A spin-off based on a bit character from the Anne of Green Gables universe. Essentially *Sabrina, the Teenage Witch*, but with bonnets.

THE BEACHCOMBERS A homely man finds logs on the beach for 387 episodes. He competes against another guy who also salvages logs. No one remembers why they liked this show, but they did.

DEGRASSI Degrassi kids can't have sex without getting AIDS and/or pregnant. They can't drink without driving a car off a roof and landing on another car in which two of their friends are having sex while getting AIDS and definitely getting pregnant. Life lesson: Do not go to Degrassi High.

Canada's most successful TV show is one long Very Special Episode.

GAME SHOWS

THE MAD DASH   Contestants won things such as "a car for one day" or cash that was literally just whatever money the host had in his pocket.

BUMPER STUMPERS   A show about guessing what a vanity license plate means. Grand prize of $1,500 that no one ever seemed to win.

PITFALL   Originally hosted by Alex Trebek. People rode an elevator while answering questions. Canada's most expensive attempt at a game show, and the production company went bankrupt, so winners never actually got the prizes and Trebek never got paid.

Half game show, half everyone's worst nightmare.

INFOBOX

For nine years the Canadian TV industry owned one camera, which all the networks had to share.

CAN YOU CON CANCON?

The CRTC (Canada's broadcasting regulator) is here to make sure Canadians get Canadian content whether they want it or not. Sixty percent of broadcast time on television stations must be dedicated to Canadian content as deemed by the CRTC.

But what makes a show Canadian? If you think simply making it in Canada means it qualifies, think again. The CRTC actually uses a point system. We can't be bothered to read it, but are fairly certain it works like this:

IS IT CANCON?

Is the producer Canadian (either a citizen, permanent resident, or actual beaver)?

☐ Yes   ☐ No

If no, then get back to America, you hoser.

_____

One director and one leading actor must be Paul Gross.

☐ Obviously

_____

Points for the following people if they are Canadian:

Director = 2 points

Lead actor = 2 points

Editor = 1 point

Guy who does the punch-up remotely = 1 point

Cousin of the grip = 0.5 points

That dog that wandered onto set = 1 point

Caterer = 0.25 points

Rick Moranis = 12 points

Based on a conceptual brainfart written on a cocktail napkin by Don McKellar or Ken Finkelstein = 3 points

TOTAL POINTS [   ]

_____

Add up total points and checkboxes and attach Jason Priestley to the project.

Note: At least 75 percent of your staff must be Eugene Levy, or Eugene Levy-adjacent (also acceptable: Jay Baruchel).

HERITAGE MOMENT

CONCERNED CHILDREN'S ADVERTISERS

THE TIME A BUNCH OF FORTUNE 500 COMPANIES JOINED FORCES TO TEACH CANADA'S CHILDREN HOW TO BE BETTER PEOPLE

In 1989, Coca-Cola, McDonald's, Nestlé, and two dozen other Fortune 500 companies decided that they were the dream team of role models for your children and formed Concerned Children's Advertisers, a Toronto-based nonprofit aimed at manipulating Canadian children into being better people.

Since then, the CCA (later renamed Companies Committed to Kids) has convinced Canada's top advertising firms to produce dozens of hallucinatory public service announcements about topics such as drug use, media literacy, and self-esteem. These spots are aired for free by Canadian broadcasters, designated as "vignettes," allowing programmers to use them to fulfill Canadian content quotas, and they have been viewed hundreds of millions of times.

COMPANIES COMMITTED TO TERRIFYING CHILDREN

HIP CHOICE (1993)

Two latex puppet children encounter a drug dealer in an alley. His hands are covered in pills and needles. They decide not to take the drugs.

DON'T YOU PUT IT IN YOUR MOUTH (1992)

Two blue fur puppets implore Canada's children not to put unknown objects into their mouths.

HOUSE HIPPO (1999)

A fake documentary about a fake species of tiny hippo that lives in Canadian homes ends with a message to Canadian children: Trust nothing you see on television.

CHOOSE A VARIETY OF FOODS (2006)

A young boy's head pops off his body. He picks up his head and uses it to grab a container of food from the fridge by his teeth. The audience is asked to "choose a variety of foods."

A Canadian filmmaker at the premiere of one of his films.

CANADIAN CINEMA

Despite the complete absence of Canadian film from Canada's movie theaters and the personal film collections of Canadians, it has long been rumored that Canadian cinema exists. There are, in fact, seven filmmakers in Canada today. They are: Atom Egoyan, Bruce McDonald, Deepa Mehta, Sarah Polley, Don McKellar, Paul Gross, and David Cronenberg. By federal decree, they are tasked with reflecting Canada on-screen. They do this by shooting their films in Canada while making sure their films avoid any reference to Canada. There are fears that overt Canadian-ing would cause an American viewer to have a nervous breakdown.

This American cinemagoer has just seen a Vancouver street sign.

CANADIAN FILM GENRES

THE SERIOUS ISSUE

War is hell. The Holocaust was terrible. Child abuse is monstrous. Give me an award.

WHITE PEOPLE IN CITIES AND CARS

Mostly they just talk to each other. Sometimes they sit in silence.

SHE HAS CANCER

Cancer is for women and it makes men sad. Being sad is a real tragedy.

IMMIGRANTS CHANGE WHITE PEOPLE'S HEARTS AND MINDS

Kindly foreign people teach a white person a lesson: Be nice to foreign people because they are kindly.

HEY, WE CAN MAKE FUN HOLLYWOOD STUFF, TOO!

No. No, we can't.

This chapter has more cool explosions than all Canadian films put together.

WHAT CHOICE DID WE HAVE?

The Canadian government paid for the following movies to be made:

P3K: PINOCCHIO 3000 (2004)

"The year is 3000. Geppetto—with the help of his faithful assistant, Spencer the cyber penguin, and the holographic fairy, Cyberina—creates Pinocchio, a prototype superrobot [sic] equipped for emotions."

MANSON, MY NAME IS EVIL (2009)

Is there any other kind of chemical engineer?

"Perry, a sheltered chemical engineer, falls in love with Leslie, a former homecoming princess (turned follower of Charles Manson), when he becomes a jury member at her hippie death cult murder trial."

SCORE: A HOCKEY MUSICAL (2010)

Love hockey? Love musicals? Oh. Well, nevermind then.

TIMELINE OF CANADIAN CINEMA

1897

Manitoba farmer James Freer shoots the first Canadian movie ever: *Arrival of CPR Express at Winnipeg*. His follow-up work is *Six Binders at Work in a Hundred-Acre Wheatfield*.

1902

The federal government gives James Freer money to tour England with his farm movies, initiating a 115-year relationship of cultural dependence on public handouts.

1911

The world's first film censorship board is founded in Ontario, begins censoring films with excessive displays of US flags as well as any films that are too good.

EDDIE: THE SLEEPWALKING CANNIBAL (2012)

A struggling Canadian artist convinces a sleepwalking cannibal to continue sleepwalking and murdering people because it's good for his art.

SPACE MILKSHAKE (2012)

"Four blue collar astronauts who are stuck together on a Sanitation Station after they bring a mysterious device aboard their ship and all life on Earth disappears . . . come under attack by a mutating rubber duck named Gary, who wants to open a portal to his evil dimension and take over the Universe."

This actually sounds pretty good.

1917	**1922**	**1939**
The Ontario Motion Picture Bureau (OMPB) is founded to create cinema that will "encourage the building of highways and other public works." Considered the high point of Canadian film. Russia launches its first state film organization the same year.	*Nanook of the North*, the world's first documentary, is shot in the Canadian Arctic. It is later found to have been almost entirely staged.	WWII begins.

Continued ⟶

Pictured: the protagonist of Porky's, a terrified glory hole.

PORKY'S

In 1974, the government tried to stimulate the Canadian film industry by making it 100 percent tax-deductible to invest money in Canadian movies. The result was an eight-year spree of low-budget C-movie schlock as dentists and realtors made zero-risk gambles to get invitations to cast parties. Canadian movies were the original offshore tax shelter: nobody on the mainland ever saw them or knew they existed. At the height of this tax-shelter era of film, Canada almost matched Hollywood for sheer volume of films released. Almost all of them were commercial flops.

Porky's *was groundbreaking because it was the only Canadian film ever to acknowledge the existence of human genitalia.*

Then there was *Porky's*. *Porky's* is a story about a group of teenagers who cause a strip club to collapse into a swamp during their quest to lose their virginity. The two main characters—Meat and Pee Wee—are named for their penises. The movie features a glory hole. The whole thing is set in Florida, which some will note is not in Canada.

For twenty-four years, *Porky's* held the record for highest-grossing Canadian film of all time.

1945
WWII ends.

1957
Nothing.

1967
Still nothing.

SHOT IN CANADA

Canadian cinema is not to be confused with "runaway" Hollywood productions filmed here to take advantage of favorable exchange rates. As a source of cheap labor for distressed projects, Canada's studios and streets have served as home to some of the worst productions ever filmed, including John Travolta's legendary Scientology-linked sci-fi atrocity *Battlefield Earth*.

This recently location-scouted Toronto street will soon be transformed into a post-apocalyptic wasteland.

1977
Anything? No?

1980
Nope.

1981
Porky's

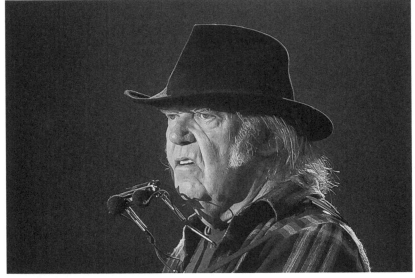

Neil Young bemoans the sorry state of MP3 recording quality during a concert.

WHINING LOSERS AND THE SOUNDS THEY MAKE

nstead of sex and rebellion, Canada's popular music is all about existential sorrow. Hipness is tragic, social scenes broken. Fun, forbidden. From the self-loathing of Leonard Cohen to the other kind of self-loathing of Drake, Canadian pop music is a pauper's grave overstuffed with the whiny (Neil Young) and the obnoxious (Barenaked Ladies). Here's a short history of Canadian pop's bummers over the past fifty-odd years.

THE 1960s

Canada birthed several of the major talents of the flower power, singer-songwriter, hippie-dippy, folk-rock generation, including Joni Mitchell and Neil Young, but they all took off for the States to find success. Canadians just aren't interested in hearing songs about the Kent State shootings, paradise being paved over, or anything remotely political or meaningful. Meanwhile, Leonard Cohen was singing about getting sad blowjobs in dingy hotel rooms. *Quel dommage!*

THE 1970s

The '70s were a banner decade for Canadian music. In 1971, Canada created the Junos, which were named after the Roman goddess Juno, but were also a nod to Canadian god Pierre Juneau, the first president of the Canadian Radio-television and Telecommunications Commission.

The '70s also saw the introduction of regulations mandating Canadian content on AM (and, later, FM) radio stations. Broadcasters were governmentally encouraged to ensure that 30 percent of their content was Canadian, leading to massive sections of airtime dedicated to Canadian artists, sometimes colloquially

Juneau himself was named after Canada's famous Juno Awards.

known as "Beaver Hour" blocks. Nothing fosters pride in one's own culture like being forced to engage with it.

An hour-long recording of actual beaver sounds would probably be more interesting than Beaver Hour radio.

One of the greatest successes of this Beaver Hour era was Toronto prog-rock outfit and Rush cover band, Rush, whose songs were often programmed to chew up large portions of the mandated Canadian content segments and who became a key part of the national rock landscape.

THE 1980s

The '80s were the era of the music video. Directly copying the success of MTV in the United States, Canada launched two television stations dedicated to music and music videos: the Toronto-based MuchMusic in 1984, and the French-language MusiquePlus, based in Montreal, in '86. Since MTV was prevented by law from broadcasting in Canada, MuchMusic was hailed as a blazingly original Canadian innovation. Also, Bryan Adams happened, but the less said about that, the better.

THE 1990s

The Barenaked Ladies' biggest contribution to culture is the theme song for the hit TV show The Big Bang Theory.

One of Canadian pop's biggest successes was a band called the Barenaked Ladies, who named their first album *Gordon* and played children's music made for adults. Alanis Morissette's bitter song about getting dumped by one of the *Full House* dads made American boys reconsider fabricating Canadian girlfriends.

Canada continued to churn out hyper-earnest balladeers throughout the decade. The best of the lot is Ron Sexsmith, who can often be spotted hauling his laundry around west-end Toronto neighborhoods. Also, Céline Dion happened, *mais moins on en dit, mieux ça vaut.*

2000s-PRESENT

The sadness, antipathy, and failure at the heart of Canadian pop music found an unlikely embodiment in Drake, the child actor turned superstar rapper turned Toronto Raptors mascot.

Despite being one of the biggest stars in the world, Drake is perpetually sullen, sorrowful, and hung up. Instead of rapping about the fruits of his success, he raps about petty decade-long grievances, group DM-ing his exes, and arguing with his girlfriend at the Cheesecake Factory.

Pictured: Drake, after being declared the greatest rapper of all time by every person in the world.

Jim Carrey's talking ass is the most famous comedy bit in Canadian history.

A PLAGUE OF WACKY ASSHOLES

Due to a glut of overconfident white men, Canada has had to extradite several to work in comedy. From Lorne Michaels to Dan Aykroyd to Tom Green, the nation has regularly shipped our best comedic talents—and Dan Aykroyd—to America. From *Austin Powers* to *Ace Ventura*, the work of Canada's top exports seems designed to feel safe, silly, and unthreatening, both to Canadians and to Americans amused by outsized kookiness and crazy costumes.

WHO?

MATCH EACH PERFORMER TO THE CLASSIC "BIT" THEY HAVE DONE:

DAN AYKROYD ·   · Fat Suit

MARTIN SHORT ·   · Talking Ass

JIM CARREY ·   · Gross Woman

MIKE MYERS ·   · Dick for a Nose

Fat Suit ⟷ Myers, Short; **Dick for a Nose** ⟷ Aykroyd; **Talking Ass** ⟷ Carrey, Myers; **Gross Woman** ⟷ Carrey, Myers

SKETCHY McSKETCHERSON

From Lenny Bruce to Richard Pryor, stand-up comedy has been a pulpit for brave truth-tellers who challenge society's hypocrisies with their strong individualistic perspectives. But give Canadians a box of wigs, a zany premise, and six or seven buddies and sure, we can be "funny."

Two Canadian TV shows have been funny: *SCTV* and *The Kids in the Hall*. They succeed where all others have failed for one reason: instead of pandering to average white Canadians, these two shows viciously destroy them.

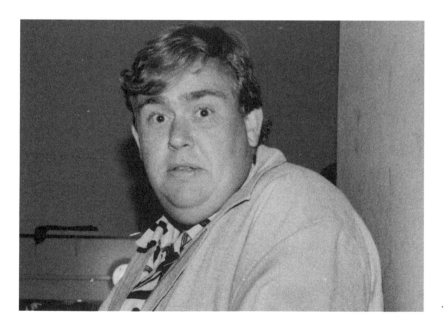

SCTV's John Candy. Season three of *SCTV* was paid for by the city of Edmonton, on the condition that production relocate to Edmonton. "People didn't want to move to Edmonton because it was Edmonton," said cast member Eugene Levy. "You don't want to be stuck in kind of a hayseed town." Citizens have since proposed an *SCTV* statue in the city.

LEACOCKIAN HUMOR

Generally speaking, Leacockian humor is the sort of comedy that benefits from being spoken into an old-timey microphone with a mildly North Atlantic accent, or—even better—shouted into a hole or pit where nobody has to hear it.

Humorist Stephen Leacock has been hailed as the Mark Twain of Canada. According to Leacock, "the best of humour is always kindly. The worst and the cheapest is malicious." For him, humor was all about "the kindly contemplation of the incongruities of life." Ha-ha, hilarious! While Leacock has been dead for a while, his legacy lives on through a number of genteel Canadian pseudo-comedies.

Corner Gas was created by Brent Butt, a guy who looks like all your dad's drinking buddies. A show about a gas station in a small town and the citizens who've gone mad from only having a gas station to go to.

CBC Radio's *Vinyl Cafe*, hosted by human cardigan Stuart McLean, who read short nostalgic essays, often about Dave and Morley, a fictional Toronto family that somehow lived off Dave's record store business.

Little Mosque on the Prairie, created by Muslim British Canadian Pakistani Zarqa Nawaz: a show about a mosque in small-town Saskatchewan that also fulfilled CBC's entire diversity quota.

QUÉBEC COMEDY

In most aspects of culture—art, cinema, food—the Québécois make Anglos look like country bumpkins. Not so in comedy. From Elvis Gratton to Oncle George to Les Boys, French Canada is locked in a Jerry Lewis-level appreciation of *les jokes*.

HILARIOUSLY UNKNOWN

RUSSELL PETERS

Brampton's Russell Peters is one of the highest-paid comedians in the world, netting over $21 million in 2013. Chris Rock called him "the most famous person nobody's ever heard of." Peters got his big break when one of his stand-up sets went viral on YouTube. But for some inexplicable reason, he is not a household name.

DASHAN

In the 1980s, U of Toronto grad Mark Rowswell got a job hosting a singing competition on Chinese television because his Chinese was really good. A white man speaking fluent Mandarin was so wild to Chinese audiences that he hosted that year's CCTV New Year's Gala, watched by 550 million. Rowswell—known in China as "Dashan"—quickly became the most recognized westerner in China by performing *xiangsheng*, a traditional form of comedic theater. Basketball star Yao Ming reportedly asked him for *his* autograph when the two met.

Peters and Dashan's "Invisible Kings of Comedy" tour sold out a 12-night run at the Rogers Centre without leaving any evidence that it had ever occurred.

One of these men will eventually try to hump this leaf.

HOW TO WRITE CANADIAN LITERATURE

ooks are important, and you should write one! Our rich tapestry of Canadian stories isn't gonna weave itself. But CanLit is a fickle beast. Here's a handy guide to help you craft your own masterpiece:

WHAT'S YOUR BOOK ABOUT? (CHOOSE ONE)

☐ Woman from city visits Southern Ontario

☐ Woman lives in Southern Ontario

☐ Man goes into wilderness

WHAT MAJOR CANADIAN THEMES WILL YOUR BOOK GRAPPLE WITH? (CHOOSE TWO)

☐ Effete City vs. Hardy, Masculine, Existential Bush

☐ Rapacious, Bad America vs. Victimized, Good Canada

WHAT MAJOR AMERICAN THEMES WILL YOUR BOOK GRAPPLE WITH? (CHOOSE AS MANY AS YOU LIKE)

☐ Sexual Liberation (Canada is a mature and progressive country!)

☐ The American Dream

☐ Feminism in America

☐ Race in America

☐ Violence

☐ The American West

☐ Environmentalism

☐ The Evils of American Consumer Culture

ADD AT LEAST TWO OF THE FOLLOWING

☐ A hardy French guy (two cultures!)

☐ Bird imagery

☐ Some honest, hardworking folks

☐ The landscape

☐ A dirty snowbank

☐ Crying birds

☐ Aboriginal symbology (no need to be an Aboriginal writer)

☐ A reluctant immigrant

The Journey Prize, the country's most prestigious award for new writers, is funded by the proceeds of James A. Michener's 1998 bestseller Journey, *considered by some people to be the worst book ever written about Canada.*

WHAT IS THE PURPOSE OF YOUR BOOK?

☐   To surprise, provoke, or—

THAT IS NOT A LEGITIMATE RESPONSE.
WHAT IS THE PURPOSE OF YOUR BOOK?

☐   To be moral and high-minded

☐   To "break barriers"

☐   To satisfy the terms of a grant

☐   I just want my book to be sold at Indigo

COULD YOUR MOM READ THIS BOOK?

Hi mom!   ☐   Yes.

TO WRITE A FUNNY BOOK ABOUT CANADA, SIMPLY TURN ANY OF THE FOLLOWING OBSERVATIONS INTO A 200-PAGE BOOK. (PLEASE SELECT ONLY FROM THIS LIST.)

☐   Canada is not an important country

☐   It is very cold in Canada!

☐   Canada has a small army

*Please make sure
you're sitting down
before you read
these!*

☐   Canadians are boring

☐   Canadians are nice

☐   Canada is big

☐   Canada has a Queen

☐   Canadian politicians are bad

☐   Toronto is bad

☐   I am from Canada

TO WRITE AN AWARD-WINNING FUNNY BOOK ABOUT CANADA, MAKE SURE TO ADD ANY OF THE FOLLOWING

- ☐ Something *en français*!

- ☐ Canadian self-deprecation (feigned and insincere)

- ☐ A reference to Pierre Trudeau's sex life

- ☐ Writing down any of these words counts as making a joke in Canadian humor writing: beer, bozo, donut, beaver, syrup, hoser, goof, any reference to hockey, any swear word

---

INFO**BOX**

CANADA READS: WHAT IS IT?

An annual radio program where Canadian celebrities fight over which book Canadians should read that year. Judges in past years: a former WWE wrestler, an astronaut, Justin Trudeau. Would be infinitely more enjoyable if the judges were made to physically fight each other with books.

CANADIAN POETRY

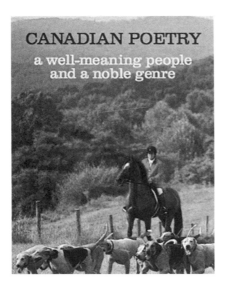

CANADIAN POETRY
a well-meaning people
and a noble genre

"Today's Canadian poetry is an adventure undertaken with brio. Its clarity and surge are evident equally whether its mood is dark or light, its pace meditative or militant. Great human hopes and debates are engaged with an openness that bespeaks humility, but with the confidence that leads an artist to firm outline, to vivid colour and movement."

—A.F. Moritz

"Do we still have a Canadian poetry? We ask this question not because Canadian poetry is an endangered species but, on the contrary, because it has never been so extraordinarily abundant and diverse."

—Studies in Canadian Literature

MAGIC
CANADIAN

EEL

POEMS OF CELEBRATION

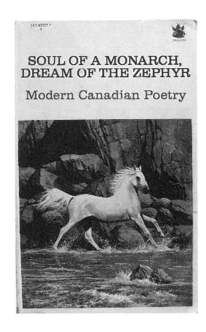

"*Canadian poetry is lyrical in form and Old English poetry is not, hence the failure to deal with sexual passion is felt as a lack in Canadian poetry but is not missed in Old English.*"

—Northrop Frye

"*Cosmopolitan, hybrid and eloquent, modern Canadian poetry is still, for many readers outside Canada, one of the great undiscovered terrains of world literature.*"

—Carcanet Press

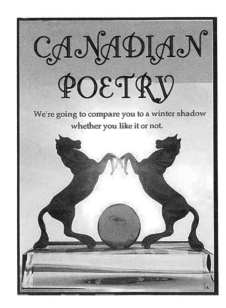

HOW WE MAKE
A LIVING

Dominion Oil CEO Robert MacFarland presides over the oil sands from his condo in downtown Calgary.

THE OIL SANDS

f there's one thing that celebrities, newspapers, and even public schools can agree on, it's that Canada's oil sands are ethical, clean, efficient, and prosperous!

Of course, the celebrities, newspapers, and public school lessons are all paid for by the oil industry. The lobby group CAPP (Canadian Association of Petroleum Producers) has been pumping cash into Canadian newspapers, magazines, billboards, and even directly into the pockets of news anchors and journalists in the form of $20,000 speaking fees.

If you would like to book Jesse to say nice things about the oil industry, please contact jesse@ canadalandshow. com.

So here's everything someone has been paid to tell you about the oil sands, directly through multimillion-dollar campaigns that have infiltrated every aspect of Canadian public life.

YUMMY!

"Bitumen has a heavy consistency similar to cold molasses or peanut butter . . . Proponents say pipelines are . . . essential projects for Canada's economy."

— "Energy IQ," a lesson plan created by the Canadian Association of Petroleum Producers and taught in hundreds of public schools

Many oil sands proponents are so attracted to bitumen that they must be physically restrained while visiting excavation sites.

"Alberta's oil sands are a responsible and sustainable major supplier of energy to the world."

— The Government of Canada, 2012 (via Bruce Carson, oil lobbyist)

"No one would be happier in the world with the oil sands being shut down than the ambassador from Saudi Arabia to Washington D.C. He would be there with his supertankers brimming with Saudi sharia oil, Saudi conflict oil, Saudi terrorist-sponsoring, women-beating oil . . . oil from Canada is the most ethical oil in the world."

— Oil lobbyist and pundit Ezra Levant

"[The oil sands] are renewing Confederation . . . You should exult in what you're doing. This is a triumph of the spirit, not something anyone should have to apologize for."

— CBC journalist and oil industry paid speaker Rex Murphy

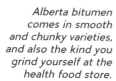

Alberta bitumen comes in smooth and chunky varieties, and also the kind you grind yourself at the health food store.

MINING AND SELLING BITUMEN

Bitumen, the mainstay of the Alberta oil industry, is a thick substance with a consistency like delicious peanut butter. It's solid at room temperature, which means that we don't have to pump it out of the ground like regular oil—we can just dig it up!

If it's deep in the ground, we might pump steam underground, making use of Canada's other natural gift, natural gas, to heat water that will melt the bitumen into a wonderful viscous semi-liquid that is easy to transport. In this process, and in purifying bitumen into something resembling oil, we employ yet another great Canadian resource—water—to wash the sand and impurities out of the oil.

All this mining, heating, pumping, and washing costs a lot of money, which makes bitumen a "luxury oil product."

INFOBOX

"Tailing ponds," the man-made lakes of toxic oil sands by-product, are collectively as large as the state of Washington.

This Alberta tree has just been released back into the wild.

RECLAIMING LAND

Alberta's responsible oil producers are on track to reclaim 100 percent of the land they dug up in search of bitumen. We haven't reclaimed any of it so far, but someday those wetlands and old-growth forests will be thriving ecosystems once more. When your grandchildren have grandchildren of their own, they'll be able to walk among fir monoculture forests so consistent, they'll wonder whether there was ever anything of value there at all.

INFOBOX

The extraction and combustion of Alberta's oil sands produces more greenhouse gas per year than the state of California.

NATURE

Picture Canada and you may imagine a vast and unspoiled woodland, a kingdom of majestic wildlife. The truth is that Canadian animals are mostly vermin, and our geography is 99 percent miserable tundra, swamp, rock, or some other sort of uninhabitable frozen wasteland.

QUOTE**SQUARE**

"The sight of the stupendous [Niagara Falls] must be one of the earliest, if not the keenest, disappointments in American married life."

—Oscar Wilde (1882)

CANADA'S GARBAGE ANIMALS

Pictured: angry bag of shit.

THE CANADA GOOSE

A giant, feathered sky insect. Regularly flies directly into the engines and windshields of airplanes. Attacks children in parks. Shits everywhere.

THE MOOSE

Huge and grotesque. Brain the size of an orange. A woodland jihadist, he wanders stupidly onto highways, where his toothpick legs crumple on impact with vehicles, sending his bulky, matted torso and antlered noggin rolling through your windshield at a deadly speed. Your last memory will be of the worst smell ever.

APPROACHING A MOOSE

Stage 1: The moose's stupid legs are destroyed.

The front of your car sweeps the moose's legs from under it, breaking them like toothpicks, but the moose's big, stupid body remains perfectly stationary due to inertia.

"Lord, let thy moose's legs stand strong against the humble grilles of our crew-cab pickups."
—Anglican Church of Canada prayer

Stage 2: The moose's stupid body enters your windshield.

A fully grown adult moose's body is positioned at exactly the height of a typical car's windshield. Instead of being obliterated by your grille like most animals, moose bodies will enter your car. It is as if the moose was designed to maximize the probability that a moose–car crash will result in the death of all moose and humans involved.

Stage 3: The moose's ridiculous-looking antlers enter your body.

If you think a moose's antlers look ridiculous when the moose is far away, think about how ridiculous they will look when they enter your body during a moose–car crash. Also look out for the moose's skull, which will probably explode on impact, and with it the moose's orange-sized brain.

THE BEAVER

Communist rodent.

THE WALRUS

Big, slow, boring. Does not deal well with criticism. Walks using its teeth. Survives via conservation efforts and a steady diet of clams. Will sometimes emit high-pitched whistling and deep moaning sounds. Generally disgusting.

The beaver is a symbol of Canada because every person in this country secretly wants to cut down a tree with their teeth, cover themselves with sticks and mud, and sleep for most of the day.

THE DEAD BABY SEAL

Guilty of attracting Paul McCartney and Anthony Bourdain to our national discourse.

In a bid to decrease international sympathy for seals, in 2005 the Nunavut government changed their name to "terrifying shark-wolves."

THE POLAR BEAR

Despite a bite force of 1,300 PSI, are wussily threatened by ice turning into water. Might as well just start calling them plain old bears at this point.

STUPID-SOUNDING ANIMALS THAT ARE THANKFULLY THREATENED OR EXTINCT

Regrettably, the Itchy-Bellied Japperbooby survives.

BANFF LONGNOSE DACE

EELGRASS LIMPET

LONGJAW CISCO

GREATER PRAIRIE CHICKEN

FROSTED ELFIN BUTTERFLY

DWARF WEDGEMUSSEL

ALBERTA'S WAR ON RATS

Albertans are so terrified of rats that in 1950 they declared war on the entire species, hammering them with poisons, fumigating them with carbon monoxide-producing engines, and even individually hunting them with firearms. Since then, the province of Alberta has declared itself the only place in the world that is entirely rat-free. Sightings of individual rats often make news in Alberta. A twenty-four-hour hotline is available to report rat sightings (310-RATS).

Each of these people has a gun pointed at their head.

CAMPING!

Camping is not only a part of our Canadian identity, it's also part of our history! When newcomers join us, we strongly insist that some of them go on long camping trips.

BANFF NATIONAL PARK, ALBERTA

In 1914, Canada forced hundreds of Ukranian Canadians to go camping in Banff and do all kinds of fun tasks, such as digging ditches, logging, mining, and helping to build Banff National Park.

SUNSHINE VALLEY, BRITISH COLUMBIA

In 1942, tens of thousands of Japanese Canadian campers were required to go camping in scenic, beautiful places in the BC interior like Sunshine Valley, for over four years.

Luckily it was the 1940s, so Canada's concentration camps still managed a one-star ranking from Frommer's.

CAMP 210 IN HOPE, BRITISH COLUMBIA

More than 170,000 single, unemployed men were sent camping in places like Camp 210 during the Depression because the government was worried they might start a communist revolution. Popular activities included clearing bush, building roads, and not being allowed to vote.

HERITAGE MOMENT

This is the only known photograph of John Holer.

JOHN HOLER

John Holer is the founder and sole owner of Marineland, Canada's most popular animal-themed amusement park. Holer says he takes better care of his animals than he does of himself, which suggests that he bleaches his bathwater and swims in his own excrement. Here are real facts about John Holer:

- Holer sold the amusement-park ride concept that would eventually become the Jules Verne Submarine ride at Disneyland, and used the money to buy two sea lions to found Marineland.

- In 1977, the Department of Fisheries seized six bottlenose dolphins that Holer was trying to smuggle into the United States from Mexico.

- In 1981, the deer at Marincland got tuberculosis. Nearly two dozen deer were eventually destroyed.

- In 1996, Holer struck a protester outside Marineland with his truck.

- According to a Marineland animal supervisor, Holer once blasted a deer non-fatally with a shotgun and drove off.

- In 2012, Holer threatened to run over a protester with his truck and "cut his head off."

- In late 2012, the Ontario Ministry of the Environment discovered Marineland was burying thousands of dead animals illegally on the property.

- In 2013, a Marineland trainer told the *Toronto Star* that Holer's tank water was causing seals to go blind and lose their skin.

- In 2013, Marineland built a massive perimeter fence, probably to keep out protesters and journalists.

- Between 2016 and 2017, Marineland was charged with 11 counts of animal cruelty towards adorable bears, elk and deer. The company has denied these charges. They also allegedly fucked-up a peacock, but who cares?

At this point maybe you are wondering, why are there deer at Marineland?

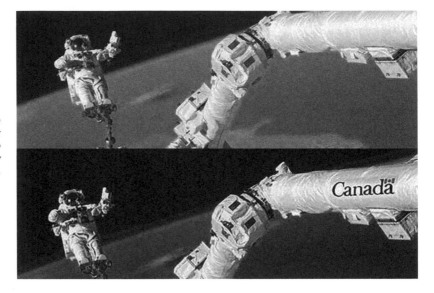

The Canadian government photoshops this logo onto anything they can find.

INVENTIONS

Canadians believe they invented many things that they did not invent. As a country that has spent most of its history drawin' water and hewin' wood, Canada should be happy with its modest contributions to the world of technology. Really! But instead it has decided to delude itself into thinking it is a modern, high-tech force.

INFO**BOX**

"Canada, a cold uncomfortable uninviting region . . . where the new inhabitants could only pass a laborious and necessitous life, in perpetual regret of the deliciousness and plenty of their native country."

—Samuel Johnson (1756)

"CANADIAN" INVENTIONS THAT ARE NOT REALLY CANADIAN

THE TELEPHONE

It is believed that Alexander Graham Bell was a Canadian who invented the telephone. He was Scottish, and he didn't. Still, various historical accounts sneak their way around this. The *Canadian Encyclopedia* cites Brantford, Ontario, as the site of the first "definitive" test of the telephone.

The CBC says that if Canada isn't the place where the telephone was invented, then it was certainly "conceived" here. After the United States House of Representatives declared Antonio Meucci the pioneer of the telephone, Canada's thirty-seventh Parliament retaliated by passing a motion insisting that Bell was the inventor.

Make sure your parents didn't conceive you here, because one day we might claim that you, too, are a Canadian invention.

THE MUSKOKA CHAIR

The Adirondack chair was invented in New York State by Thomas Lee in 1903. But in Canada people call them Muskoka chairs and credit them to the shrubby, overpriced cottage country north of Toronto.

BASKETBALL

James A. Naismith invented basketball. He invented it in Massachusetts. He was from Ontario, and historical revisionists struggling to find Canadian roots for his American invention say that as a child in Ontario Naismith played a game called duck on a rock. Duck on a rock is a medieval stone-throwing game that also isn't Canadian and is nothing like basketball.

THE SNOWMOBILE

This one must be Canadian, right? Wrong. In 1916, Ray H. Muscott of Michigan was granted a US patent for the "motor sleigh," which used a track-and-ski design similar to modern snowmobiles at least twelve years before Joseph-Armand Bombardier even thought of the idea.

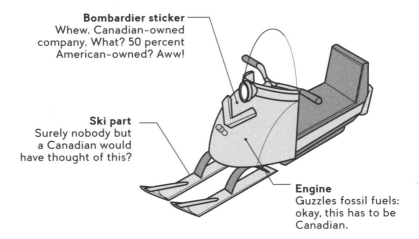

Bombardier sticker
Whew. Canadian-owned company. What? 50 percent American-owned? Aww!

Ski part
Surely nobody but a Canadian would have thought of this?

Engine
Guzzles fossil fuels: okay, this has to be Canadian.

THE CANADARM

Since the dawn of time, the greatest visionaries of the human race have dreamed of space travel. When they finally achieved this goal, the greatest visionaries of Canada said, "How will we hug aliens?" The Canadarm has already flown on more than ninety space shuttle missions, but its greatest service was in providing a cover image for every Canadian science textbook ever published.

HERITAGE MOMENT

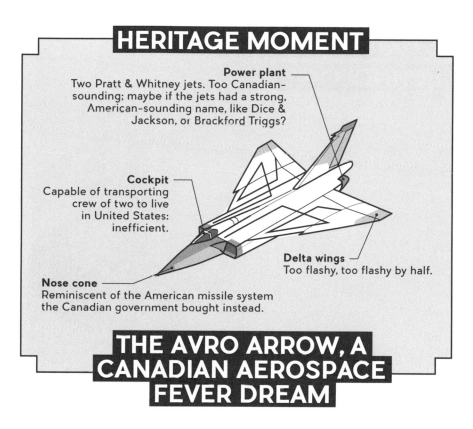

Power plant
Two Pratt & Whitney jets. Too Canadian-sounding; maybe if the jets had a strong, American-sounding name, like Dice & Jackson, or Brackford Triggs?

Cockpit
Capable of transporting crew of two to live in United States: inefficient.

Delta wings
Too flashy, too flashy by half.

Nose cone
Reminiscent of the American missile system the Canadian government bought instead.

THE AVRO ARROW, A CANADIAN AEROSPACE FEVER DREAM

The apex of Canadian technological achievement in the twentieth century was an airplane we never finished. The Avro Arrow was a Cold War-era nation-building project; it was a chance for Canada to produce the greatest interceptor jet in aviation history. But it was suddenly canceled by the prime minister in 1959 with no reason given, and 30,000 of the best engineers and scientists in the world were laid off. Many left the country. All was not lost, though, as a 1997 TV movie about the failed project was successfully produced. It starred Dan Aykroyd.

ACTUAL CANADIAN TECHNOLOGY

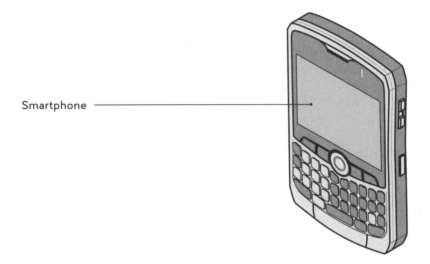

Smartphone

THE SMARTPHONE

Canada's greatest contribution to electronics is also its most embarrassing failure. We had the smartphone first by way of Research In Motion (Waterloo, Ontario), which beat Apple to market by eight years. The BlackBerry by RIM sold millions of devices to business users. It was the de facto mobile Internet device for years. But RIM didn't think regular folks would need or want such sophisticated gadgets. They didn't think their business users would ever trade in tiny, tiny keyboards for touchscreens. They didn't think letting other companies make apps for their phones was such a hot idea. They are now an insignificant player in a $219 billion market that they created.

THE GARBAGE BAG

Harry Wasylyk (Winnipeg, Manitoba) and Larry Hanson (Lindsay, Ontario) invented the first polyethylene garbage bag in 1950, initially marketing the product to hospitals. They sold the patent to Union Carbide, who created the Glad brand in the 1960s. Assumedly, mass-producing plastic bags was beyond the capabilities of Canadian industry.

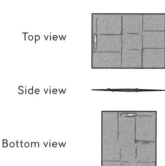

Top view

Side view

Bottom view

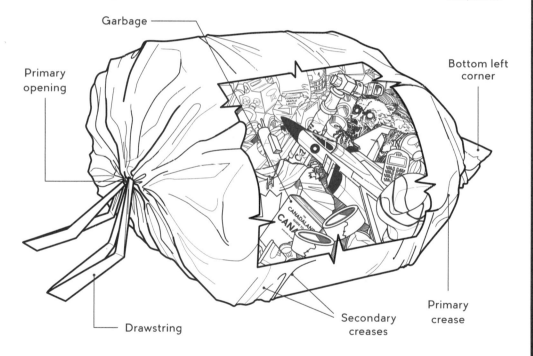

Garbage

Primary opening

Bottom left corner

Drawstring

Secondary creases

Primary crease

Primary garbage bag chamber

Polyethylene body

HIGHER EDUCATION

Canada's postsecondary schools are world-class adult daycare centres, where extended adolescents can learn basic life skills like how to drink and how to be fleeced by an institution while thinking that they are fleecing an institution. While they remain packed to capacity during the day, most of these facilities empty out after six p.m., when it is time for students to commute home and climb back into their mothers' wombs. Many of these schools have resorted to tricking foreign students into thinking that they can use their degrees to get jobs or permanent Canadian residency.

POPULAR BACK-TO-SCHOOL ACTIVITIES

FLIPPING OVER AND SETTING FIRE TO CARS

In 2005, students attending Queen's University's Homecoming event rioted, flipping over and setting fire to a car and chanting, "Fuck the police," while riot squads began arresting dozens of people. After banning the event, Queen's brought it back in 2013.

SONGS ABOUT RAPE

In 2013, students at the University of British Columbia and Saint Mary's University in Halifax were heard enthusiastically chanting about nonconsensual sex with underage girls. In 2011, Queen's University's marching band, Canada's largest and oldest, published copies of a secret internal pamphlet containing phrases such as "I will rape you with a lamp," "Mouth raping your little sister since 1905," and "Perpetuating racial stereotypes since 1905."

Queen's University took this opportunity to quietly change their motto from "Perpetuating racial stereotypes since 1905."

BLACKFACE

In 2011, fifteen students at a frosh week initiation event at Montreal's HEC business school dressed up in blackface and chanted about smoking "more weed," which they claimed was an homage to Olympic runner Usain Bolt.

THE MOST TERRIBLE THINGS YOU CAN THINK OF, IF YOU'RE AT DALHOUSIE AND IT'S 2015

In 2015, it was revealed that thirteen men from the Dalhousie School of Dentistry had started a Facebook group that discussed which female classmates they wanted to chloroform and "hate fuck." The same year, a Dalhousie medical student was charged with first-degree murder in the death of a fellow student, and another Dalhousie medical student was found with two guns and 1,834 rounds of ammunition after allegedly threatening to kill a dean, twenty other students, and himself. (The charges were eventually dropped, and the student was served with a peace bond and restricted from owning any weapons.)

EMBRACING DIVERSITY

Just kidding. In 2010, an investigation by *Maclean's* magazine found that many affluent white Canadians actively avoid enrolling at schools with a high concentration of "Asian" students (*Maclean's* did not specify whether this means Canadian-born Chinese-, Japanese-, and Korean-Canadians; immigrants; or international students from Asian countries, or whether the magazine was itself also being racist).

"All the white kids go to Queen's, Western and McGill," reports Alexandra, "a second-year student who looks like a girl from an Aritzia billboard."

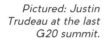

Pictured: Justin Trudeau at the last G20 summit.

CANADA'S TOP UNIVERSITIES ACCORDING TO THEIR ALUMNI

McGILL: JUSTIN TRUDEAU

While at McGill, Trudeau was known for gliding between classrooms in a pair of Rollerblades. McGill's reputation, like Trudeau's, is more about name recognition than excellence. McGill's mascot, Marty the Martlet, is a mythical bird that can never land because he doesn't have any feet and therefore spends all his time flying higher: a symbol for desperate striving. Trudeau's mascot, a Haida raven tattooed on his shoulder, is a symbol of the prime minister's desperate desire for people to like him.

UNIVERSITY OF WATERLOO: MIKE LAZARIDIS

At age twelve, Lazaridis won an award for reading every science book at his local public library. Six years later, he enrolled at the University of Waterloo. He

Waterloo is like Canada's MIT, if MIT were filled with people who didn't get into MIT.

ended up dropping out to launch Research In Motion (BlackBerry), proving that obtaining a degree from Waterloo actually decreases your chances of creating a successful tech company. Like his Waterloo classmates, Lazaridis's life goal is to convert as much nerd rage as he can into usable code.

QUEEN'S UNIVERSITY: EVERY FUCKING BANKER AND CEO

Queen's alumni have gone on to occupy executive positions at hundreds of companies, including the Royal Bank of Canada, UBS, Ontario Teachers' Pension Plan, Pizza Pizza, Sleep Country Canada, Torstar, American Airlines, and MasterCard. Most of them were probably put through university by their parents, who likely also went to Queen's and worked in finance or business, and most of them would probably be delighted if you called them entitled, privileged elitists.

UNIVERSITY OF BRITISH COLUMBIA: THE OWNER OF THIS BEAUTIFUL McLAREN 650S SPIDER

At any given point in time, the campus of the University of British Columbia in Vancouver is teeming with dozens of cars like this one. The eighteen-year-old owners of these $300,000+ supercars are likely very well adjusted and will totally grow up to be humble non-elitists, for sure, no question about that.

Queen's University-style car-flipping would definitely not fly at UBC.

JULIE'S HEALTH CARE ADVENTURE

ASK CANADIANS WHAT THEY LIKE BEST ABOUT THEIR HOMELAND AND THERE'S A GOOD CHANCE THEY'LL SAY IT'S THE FACT THAT WE HAVE UNIVERSAL HEALTH CARE!

EVERY CANADIAN KNOWS THAT WE HAVE THE BEST HEALTHCARE SYSTEM IN THE WESTERN HEMISPHERE. THIS SOUNDS IMPRESSIVE UNTIL YOU CONSIDER THE COMPETITION, WHICH INCLUDES THE USA, ARGENTINA, BRAZIL, NICARAGUA, COLOMBIA, AND HAITI. ALSO, SUCK IT, SAMOA! WE'RE #1.

DON'T JUST TAKE OUR WORD FOR IT. POOR HYPOTHETICAL JULIE JUST HURT HER ARM FALLING OFF HER BIKE. HER BAD FORTUNE IS YOUR OPPORTUNITY TO SEE JUST HOW EFFECTIVE AND EFFICIENT A CANADIAN HOSPITAL CAN BE.

JULIE HAS BROKEN HER ARM. LUCKY HER! TIME TO ENJOY YOUR SHARE OF FREE HEALTH CARE.

JULIE IS ON HER WAY TO A "P3" (PUBLIC-PRIVATE-PARTNERSHIP) HOSPITAL. THAT'S WHERE THE GOVERNMENT PAYS A COMPANY TO DO THINGS LIKE BUILD HOSPITALS AND RUN BASIC GOVERNMENT FUNCTIONS AT A HYPER-INFLATED COST.

AFTER BUILDING A P3 HOSPITAL, THE GOVERNMENT ALSO PAYS A LEASE FOR IT AND PAYS A COMPANY TO OPERATE IT. BY PAYING THREE TIMES, THE GOVERNMENT CREATES JOBS!

IN 2014, 27 PERCENT OF CANADIANS REPORTED WAITING FOR FOUR HOURS IN A HOSPITAL WAITING ROOM. WITH TIME TO SPARE, JULIE CAN MAKE FRIENDS!

CANADA'S 77,000 DOCTORS MAKE $225,000 A YEAR ON AVERAGE. JULIE'S DOCTOR CONCLUDES THAT HER ARM IS BROKEN. HE WILL BE BACK IN THREE HOURS!

14 HOURS LATER, JULIE LEAVES WITH A PRESCRIPTION AND AN APPOINTMENT WITH A SPECIALIST IN FOUR MONTHS. HER ARM WILL TAKE TWO MONTHS TO HEAL.

LET'S HOPE JULIE'S PARENTS ARE INSURED BECAUSE THEY WILL HAVE TO PAY OVER $1,000 FOR PRESCRIPTIONS, AN AMBULANCE RIDE, AND PHYSIO.

JULIE IS NOW RESTING AT HOME WITH HER ARM ON THE MEND! GOOD, 'CAUSE TOMORROW SHE'LL BE BACK AT THE HOSPITAL TO DEAL WITH THE INFECTION SHE CAUGHT IN THE WAITING ROOM.

Vancouver is a hermit kingdom, separated from reality by the Rocky Mountains to the east and the Pacific Ocean to the west. In its isolation, Vancouver has gone insane and lost all frame of reference, and locals are consistently in one kind of fantasy stupor or another. Come for a visit soon, as a massive earthquake is expected to jolt Vancouverites back to reality any day now.

WHO YOU'LL MEET

JUNKIES

Vancouver's Downtown Eastside is home to a sobering number of heroin addicts, and a visit to any Hastings alleyway will mortify even the most hardened street-dweller. "This is terrible," remarked a scandalized Snoop Dogg in a 2016 Instagram video as his SUV drove over piles of syringes. "You need to clean this shit up."

TEENAGE MILLIONAIRES

Nouveau-riche Chinese (also Indians, Iranians, and Saudis) send their offspring to Vancouver, where they reside in swanky homes and drive expensive cars.

TEENAGE MILLIONAIRE STARTUP FOUNDERS

Huffing the northward-drifting fumes of Silicon Valley, local gurus and thinkfluentials all want to score big with the next Hootsuite or PlentyofFish. Know what Retsly, Zeetl, Tingle, or Yiip do? That's okay, neither do their employees.

SPORTY ENLIGHTENED HIPPIES

All other Vancouverites are fitness-crazed, Eastern philosophy-loving, fleece-wearing, real estate-speculating hippies.

WHERE TO GO

KITSILANO

A charming middle-class neighborhood, popular with young parents, filled with parks, beaches, and beautiful heritage homes, all of which will be wiped off the face of the earth by a cataclysmic 8.0+ "megaquake."

YALETOWN

Formerly the city's rail yard, Yaletown has been transformed into a neighborhood filled with trendy bars, parks, spas, and boutiques, and is set to be transformed again when, as one scientist put it, an earthquake "rips the earth open like a zipper" and kills thousands of people in a matter of seconds.

GASTOWN

Home to some of the city's most popular historic sites, restaurants, profit-free tech startups, and least earthquake-resistant buildings. It will not be spared in the destruction.

Pictured: Bill Clinton jogging along the Vancouver Seawall.

ENEMIES OF VANCOUVER

DAVID DUCHOVNY

After shooting *The X-Files* in Vancouver in 1997, Duchovny told late-night TV host Conan O'Brien that "Vancouver is a very nice city if you like four hundred inches of rainfall a day." Like any other world-class city would, Vancouver responded by holding a two-decade-long grudge against David Duchovny.

BIKE THIEVES

If caught stealing a bike in Vancouver, be prepared to fight lions in Rogers Arena or to be crucified along Broadway Street.

ANYONE WITH BASIC HUMAN DECENCY

Vancouver has more homeless people than anywhere else in Canada. It also has more empty homes than anywhere else in Canada, in an effort to give homeless people something to aspire to.

Warren G. Harding became the first sitting US president to visit Canada when he slipped over the border to Vancouver for a day. He spoke to cheering crowds at Stanley Park, went golfing in Richmond, and developed a nasty cough. Five days later, the cough killed him. He remains the only US president to die from visiting Vancouver (so far).

WHAT TO DO IN THE WORLD'S MOST INTENSELY LAID-BACK CITY

MASOCHISM

"Laid-back" Vancouverites like to brag about how in Vancouver you can go to work, walk along the beach, hike up a mountain, and go skiing all in one day. If you also enjoy torture, consider the Grouse Grind, a three-kilometer run straight up the side of a mountain! In 2013, a Vancouver teenager ran up the Grind a record sixteen times in one day, assumedly to sweat off the shame of impure thoughts. In 2015, a fifty-five-year-old man died of a heart attack while doing the Grind. Zealots pay tribute to his martyrdom daily.

TAKE A DELICIOUS SHOT OF HEROIN IN FRONT OF A POLICE OFFICER

Vancouver's government-funded safe injection site, Insite, is one of the only public places in the world where you can do heroin with an attentive audience.

DRINK

Vancouverites have very strict bedtimes: nine p.m. on weekdays and eleven p.m. on weekends (at the latest). Vancouver bars and restaurants are not yet required by law to call your mother if they see you out past these times. Vancouverites were not allowed to drink on Sundays until 1986, when Prince Charles and Princess Diana visited the city for Expo 86 and desperately needed a drink.

GETTING AROUND

THE PLIGHT OF VANCOUVER'S SUPERCAR OWNERS

Vancouver is a walkable, environmentally friendly city, which makes life tough for the city's supercar owners (the largest per capita in North America). This is their struggle:

- Not being able to fit their backpack, textbooks, and laundry into the trunk of your neon-green 2014 Lotus Elise.

- Getting constantly pulled over by cops just so they can admire the car.

- Fucking up the air intake of their 2012 Fisker Karma after driving 125 km/h through Pacific Spirit Park and hitting a fox.

- Getting their Audi RS5 scratched after they accidentally parked in the Downtown Eastside, one of Canada's poorest postal codes.

- The fact that there are so many other supercars in Vancouver, rendering theirs not so super.

GLOBAL WARMING?
FUCK YEAH!

Climate change is already pushing the globe into a state of permanent crisis characterized by food riots, climate refugees, civil wars, drought, famine, disease, tsunamis, hurricanes, and general catastrophe. Not in Canada. It's not just that we're far from all the suffering. The truth is, it helps us. That's why we've been nudging it along.

WHY GLOBAL WARMING IS AWESOME FOR CANADA

OUR CLIMATE IS TERRIBLE AND WE'D LIKE TO CHANGE IT

Canada's shitty weather has already improved. Toronto in 2017 feels kinda like New York in 1993—you still need a winter coat, but now it can be stylish instead of a duvet with arm holes. Homes require less winter heating. As such, we're starting to creep our cities northwards into the vast (vast, vast) reserves of land we've previously avoided or just sucked resources from.

ALL THAT ICE WAS GETTING IN THE WAY OF STUFF

Speaking of resources, arctic thaw will soon grant us access to the vast reserves of natural gas trapped beneath the North Pole. Also, the Northwest Passage is finally navigable, so we've got that going for us too.

WE'LL HAVE MORE OF THE THINGS EVERYONE ELSE WILL HAVE LESS OF

Our fossil fuels become more and more valuable as the world's energy reserves deplete. Plus we've got lots of water, which is about to become a very big deal.

WE LIVE IN A SAFE NEIGHBORHOOD

Our hyper-militarized allies to the south will fend off encroaching marauders from have-not nations.

ON THE OTHER HAND...

True, we may lose some cities to rising sea levels. But we've already sold most of Vancouver to the global super-rich anyhow.

DO NOT BELIEVE CANADIANS WHEN THEY TALK ABOUT GLOBAL WARMING

"When it comes to our environment, we Canadians get it." —Justin Trudeau

In 2015, Canada had the third-worst environmental protection record in the world, according to the Centre for Global Development.

"We'll protect our wildlife and our water." —Justin Trudeau

We got a "D" grade on air pollution and freshwater management in an independent review of environmental performance.

"We need to take real action on climate change." —Justin Trudeau

Canada has the worst climate change record in the developed world, according to Climate Action Network Europe.

This is Canada's current climate change strategy.

WHAT WE SAY WHEN WE THINK NOBODY ELSE IS LISTENING

"Global warming will hurt most economies, but boost Canada's."

—CBC News

"Canada is looking hot!"

—*Toronto Sun*

"By the year 2050 Canada could be enjoying newfound status as a global superpower blessed with a developed north, plenty of fresh water, a growing population and new shipping lanes through the Arctic."

—CTV News

"Opportunities: [global] warming may provide opportunities for agriculture. Warmer temperatures would also benefit livestock production. Climate change could improve soil quality."

—Agriculture Canada

QUOTESQUARE

"I love Canada."

—Donald Trump

THE WALL

It's 2021: Post-wall Mexico is thriving. With Industrial Age factory jobs back in the US, Mexico has had to refocus and has become the world's new tech hub ("El Silicon Grande"). Trump needed a new country to blame for his reelection bid, so he picked Canada and it worked. Introducing the Canadian Friendship Enhancement Barrier.

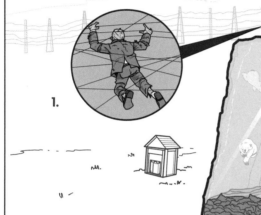

CONSTRUCTION

The wall is made of ice, our most abundant resource, as well as bitumen, unpaid interns, and all of Canada's polar bears. When the atmosphere and economy are fixed, all animals and interns will be thawed and revived. Original Daniel Libeskind design called for glass, but we ran out of money.

SECURITY

On the Canadian side, there are sheds every 300 meters with signs reading "Welcome to Canada. Free health care and marijuana right in here." When border jumpers step inside a shed, the door latches behind them and they are then arrested.

TUNNELS

Canadians use these to smuggle in good movies and visiting NHL and NBA teams. The tunnels are also used to smuggle out Lena Dunham whenever she makes it in.

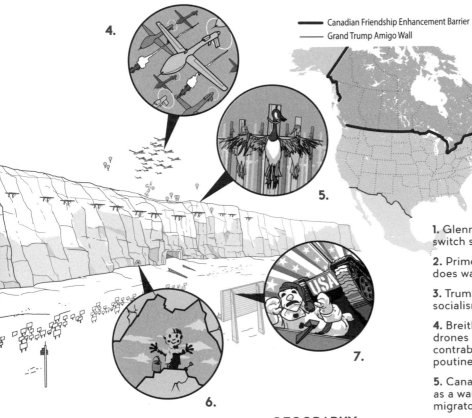

Canadian Friendship Enhancement Barrier
Grand Trump Amigo Wall

1. Glenn Beck tries, fails to switch sides

2. Prime Minister Trudeau does wall duty

3. Trump voters keep socialism out of America

4. BreitbartRT™ newsbattle drones hunt down contraband UberEats poutine delivery bots

5. Canada geese crucified as a warning to other migratory birds

6. Inane Banksy mural

7. US anti-Bonhomme propaganda

PROPAGANDA

On the US side, loudspeakers blare propaganda featuring Canadian-born celebrities expressing their love for the United States. "I am happy here. America is great again," screams a brainwashed Jim Carrey.

GEOGRAPHY

Due to clerical error, New Brunswick was fenced on the US side. Detroit has erected a two-dimensional Potemkin Village along the Canadian border so that the city looks glitzy and revitalized. With no money for a wall between Alaska and the Yukon, both sides have resorted to simply shooting everyone else who lives there.

FINALLY SPECIAL

Post-NAFTA, tariffs on Hollywood fare force Canada to actually create its own culture. Proves too difficult, so everyone finally learns French and watches Québec reality TV instead.

IMAGE CREDITS